Autism Methodology Cases to Live by:

Legal Guidance for Practical Program Strategies

Elena M. Gallegos, Esq.

Jill M. Shallenberger, Esq.

Publications

LRP Publications
Horsham, Pennsylvania 19044

This publication was designed to provide accurate and authoritative information in regard to the subject matter covered. It is published with the understanding that neither the author nor the publisher is engaged in rendering legal, accounting, or other professional service. If legal advice or other expert assistance is required, the service of a competent professional should be sought.

Library of Congress Cataloging-in-Publication Data

Gallegos, Elena M. (Elena Martinez)
   Autism methodology cases to live by : legal guidance for practical program strategies /
by Elena M. Gallegos and Jill M. Shallenberger.
        p. cm.
     Includes bibliographical references.
     ISBN 1-57834-100-0
   1. Autistic children--Education--United States. 2. Autistic children--Education--Law
and legislation--United States. 3. Asperger's syndrome. 4. Autism. I. Shallenberger,
Jill M. II. Title.

   LC4718.G35   2008
   371.94--dc22

                                                                                            2008012803

About the Authors

ELENA MARTINEZ GALLEGOS, Esq., heads the Albuquerque office of Walsh, Anderson, Brown, Schulze & Aldridge, P.C., where she is a longtime shareholder. She has practiced with the firm since graduating from the University of Texas School of Law in 1988. Ms. Gallegos is licensed to practice law in Texas and New Mexico. A former special education teacher, her practice emphasizes special education issues. From 2000-2005, she served as a program specialist with the Mountain Plains Regional Resource Center, which is funded by the U.S. Department of Education's Office of Special Education Programs to provide technical assistance to state departments of education in 10 states and the Bureau of Indian Affairs. She has served on the board of directors of the Education Law Association and speaks nationally on issues of school law.

JILL M. SHALLENBERGER, Esq., is a briefing attorney in the Albuquerque office of Walsh, Anderson, Brown, Schulze & Aldridge, P.C. She is a 2003 graduate of Stanford University Law School. A former textbook editor and middle school teacher, she has worked as an attorney primarily in the field of education law, both in private practice and as an assistant general counsel with the New Mexico Public Education Department. Ms. Shallenberger is licensed to practice law in New Mexico. Her practice emphasizes research and writing in all areas of school law.

Table of Contents

Acknowledgment

We owe our gratitude to Nathan Wilson, a University of New Mexico law student and a law clerk for the Walsh Anderson law firm during the time that this book was written. A father of four and a former special education teacher, Mr. Wilson dedicated enormous time, skill, thoughtful insight, and good humor to the project at all stages of its development, and his contribution is deeply appreciated.

Introduction

The number of children in the United States diagnosed with an autism spectrum disorder (ASD) is rising:

> According to the Autism Society of America, about 1.5 million Americans are currently living with some form of autism. This figure includes more than 100,000 school-aged children diagnosed with autism served under the Individuals with Disabilities Education Act (IDEA). . . .[1]

> Recent estimates of the prevalence of ASDs are in the range of 6.5 to 6.6 per 1,000. . . .[2]

The challenges associated with educating children with autism spectrum disorders are increasingly being felt by public schools, which are required to provide a "free appropriate public education" (FAPE) to children with disabilities under the federal Individuals with Disabilities Education Act (IDEA). Among these challenges are those of designing a program and selecting and implementing appropriate instructional methodologies, particularly given the fierce debates within the educational community that have ensued in recent years regarding educational methodologies for children with autism spectrum disorders. Against this backdrop, the National Research Council has stated:

> Many disputes arise because of the uncertainties of the various parties about what is appropriate and available in individual circumstances. It would be useful for all concerned to have an updated summary of current case law on cases with children with autistic spectrum disorders . . . so that schools and parents can understand the various options available to them that are consistent with FAPE. Policies are always evolving as new knowledge and problems are introduced into the environment. The professional community that wishes to stand with the parents and the needs of their children should not be placed in an antagonistic posture to them by rules and regulations that hinder rather than help the positive relationship between school and family.[3]

This book is intended to respond to this call for greater information and clarity of understanding. Specifically, our goal is to provide public school educators with guidelines gleaned from key cases[4] to help prepare them to address the autism methodology debate in a manner that is both educationally sound and legally defensible.

ENDNOTES

[1] U.S. Government Accountability Office. *Special education: Children with autism*, 1. Washington, D.C., January 2005.

[2] Myers, Scott M., M.D. (2007). Management of children with autism spectrum disorders. *Pediatrics,* vol. 120: num. 5 (Nov. 2007): 1162.

[3] National Research Council. (2001). *Educating children with autism.* Committee on Educational Interventions for Children with Autism. Catherine Lord and James P. McGee, eds. Division of Behavioral and Social Sciences and Education. Washington, D.C.: National Academy Press.

[4] Many of the cases discussed in this book will receive treatment in multiple chapters and will be examined on several different levels throughout the book.

Chapter 1

A Historical Overview of the Leading Methodology Cases

From a legal perspective, sound, broad-based programming by school districts for children with autism spectrum disorders increases the likelihood that courts will show deference to the district's instructional methodology choices, regardless of what those choices are. Our emphasis on sound programming regardless of chosen methodology is grounded in both the historical and current case law concerning methodology disputes. The focus of this chapter is a historical overview of the leading cases on methodology.

To provide a context for these cases, we begin with a review of the underlying statutory framework of the IDEA. The IDEA guarantees to every child with a disability the right to a free appropriate public education, or FAPE.

The federal regulations define "FAPE" as follows:

> *Free appropriate public education or FAPE* means special education and related services that —
>
> (a) Are provided at public expense, under public supervision and direction, and without charge;
>
> (b) Meet the standards of the SEA, including the requirements of this part;
>
> (c) Include an appropriate preschool, elementary school, or secondary school education in the State involved; and
>
> (d) Are provided in conformity with an individualized education program (IEP) that meets the requirements of §§300.320 through 300.324.

34 CFR 300.17.

These regulations also define "special education" as:

> [S]pecially designed instruction, at no cost to the parents, to meet the unique needs of a child with a disability. . . .

34 CFR 300.39(a)(1).

"Specially designed instruction" means:

> [A]dapting, as appropriate to the needs of an eligible child under this part, the content, *methodology*, or delivery of instruction —
>
> (i) To address the unique needs of the child that result from the child's disability; and
>
> (ii) To ensure access of the child to the general curriculum, so that the child can meet

the educational standards within the jurisdiction of the public agency that apply to all children.

34 CFR 300.39(b)(3) (emphasis added).

Board of Education v. Rowley

In *Board of Education v. Rowley*, 553 IDELR 656 (EHLR 553:656), 458 U.S. 176 (1982), which involved a dispute over the delivery of interpreter services for a child who was profoundly deaf, the U.S. Supreme Court set forth the defining standard for determining FAPE as a two-part test:

> First, has the State complied with the procedures set forth in the Act? And second, is the individualized educational program developed through the Act's procedures reasonably calculated to enable the child to receive educational benefits? If these requirements are met, the State has complied with the obligations imposed by Congress and the courts can require no more.

The Court also stated:

> Insofar as a State is required to provide a [disabled] child with a "free appropriate public education," we hold that it satisfies this requirement by providing personalized instruction with sufficient support services to permit the child to benefit educationally from that instruction.

The *Rowley* court declined to establish a fixed rule for determining the quantum of educational benefit that must be conferred, but did conclude that, "while an IEP need not maximize the potential of a disabled student, it must provide 'meaningful' access to education, and confer 'some educational benefit' upon the child for whom it is designed."[1]

Some circuits have since interpreted this standard to require that an IEP offer "meaningful benefit"[2] and "more than a trivial or de minimis educational benefit,"[3] to be "gauged in relation to the potential of the child at issue."[4] While the IDEA is intended "to open the door of public education to [disabled] children," it is not intended "to guarantee any particular level of education once inside."[5] However, states are free to establish a higher standard than the federal minimum.[6] In addition, the *Rowley* court articulated the distinct roles of courts and educators with respect to educational methodology debates:

> In assuring that the requirements of the Act have been met, courts must be careful to avoid imposing their view of preferable educational methods upon the States. The primary responsibility for formulating the education to be accorded a [disabled] child, and for choosing the educational method most suitable to the child's needs, was left by the Act to state and local educational agencies in cooperation with the parents or guardian of the child.
>
> . . . Therefore, once a court determines that the requirements of the Act have been met, questions of methodology are for resolution by the States.

The *Rowley* Standard, Applied to Methodology Disputes

When adjudicating methodology disputes, courts since *Rowley* have consistently refrained from "'substitut(ing) their own notions of sound educational policy for those of the school authorities which they review.'"[7] The following case excerpt articulates the widely accepted extent of the court's authority in adjudicating such disputes:

> Neither a state administrative hearing officer nor a reviewing court may reject an otherwise appropriate IEP because of dissatisfaction with the educational methodology proposed in the IEP. If an IEP is "reasonably calculated to enable the child to receive educational benefits," the hearing officer cannot reject it because the officer believes that a different methodology would be better for the child.[8]

Put another way, courts are tasked with determining whether a district's IEP is reasonably calculated to provide a FAPE. If they determine that it is, the district has satisfied the IDEA's requirements and the court will not second-guess the district's methodology choice.

Many influential methodology cases have involved children with hearing impairments. For example, *Lachman v. Illinois State Board of Education*, 441 IDELR 156 (EHLR 441:156), 852 F.2d 290 (7th Cir. 1988), *cert. denied*, 488 U.S. 925 (1988), has guided federal court decisions in numerous methodology cases concerning children with autism spectrum disorders.

Mr. and Mrs. Lachman sought assistance from the Regional Hearing Impaired Program (RHIP) when they discovered that Benjamin was profoundly deaf at 10 months of age. The program used the total communication methodology to teach communication through sign language, finger spelling, and simultaneous talking. Before age 2, Benjamin began speech and language services using total communication. His parents, however, grew frustrated by the differences between Benjamin's language skills and those of hearing children. They also were frustrated by the method because Mr. Lachman experienced difficulty with learning sign language and adapting to its use.

The Lachmans began searching for alternatives to help Benjamin. An independent evaluation confirmed their concerns about his significantly delayed skills. They learned about cued speech from a RHIP teacher and attended a workshop about the method. They learned that it was more easily implemented than sign language, using only eight hand shapes formed in four positions near the mouth. The hand shapes were used to clarify phonic ambiguities and enhance lip-reading. The Lachmans began using cued speech with Benjamin, became proficient in the method, and discontinued using sign language.

Cued speech gave the Lachmans the results for which they were searching. A second independent evaluation showed that Benjamin improved in language comprehension after using the method for eight months. Just five months later, when Benjamin was 3, a third independent evaluation showed that he had approached or exceeded language comprehension levels of children with normal hearing.

At age 3, Benjamin became eligible for school-based services provided by a RHIP contract with his school district. The school-based program used total communication to integrate language instruction with every subject throughout the school day. The program also was investigating the cued speech method through a pilot program. At the time, RHIP served 75 children from 47 school districts and was regarded as one of the best in the country.

Benjamin's special education needs were evaluated at age 3 and again at age 4. Following each evaluation, the district recommended that Benjamin be educated using total communication. The Lachmans rejected the plan both times because it did not employ their preferred method, cued speech. Instead, they enrolled him in a private school and employed a cued speech translator to accompany Benjamin at the private school. His teacher reported that he performed the regular class curriculum as well as most of his peers.

As Benjamin approached age 5, his parents requested that he attend a regular kindergarten classroom in his neighborhood school accompanied by an experienced cued speech interpreter. The district proposed an IEP that would provide a cued speech interpreter for half of the school day and the RHIP total communication program for the other half. The Lachmans claimed that sign language was an inappropriate method, rejected the plan, and requested a due process hearing. Both the Level I and the Level II due process hearing officers upheld the IEP. The parents appealed the case to federal district court.

The school district and the Lachmans continued their efforts to resolve the dispute while awaiting appearance in district court. Within months, they agreed that Benjamin should be reevaluated in a regular kindergarten classroom in his neighborhood school with the support of a cued speech interpreter. District education professionals used information gathered during the four-week evaluation period to choose methods designed to provide Benjamin with a FAPE. Teacher observations, a speech and language evaluation, and a psychological evaluation were completed during the reevaluation. Another IEP was developed and the district again recommended total communication as the method that would meet his educational needs. The IEP also included the use of cued speech for a brief time to assist him with the transition to sign language. The Lachmans remained convinced that sign language was an inappropriate method for Benjamin. Unsatisfied with the proposed use of total communication in the IEP, they maintained their appeal before the district court.

Before the district court, the Lachmans used expert witnesses to try to prove that cued speech should be used to teach Benjamin. However, the court disagreed, concluding that the district had carefully considered his educational needs and had offered him a FAPE. Standing their ground that Benjamin should only be taught through cued speech, the Lachmans appealed the decision to the 7th Circuit Court of Appeals. The 7th Circuit also disagreed with the parents, stating that:

> parents, no matter how well-motivated, do not have a right under the EAHCA [the Education for All Handicapped Children Act, the precursor to the IDEA] to compel a school district to provide a specific program or employ a specific methodology in providing for the education of their [disabled] child.

The court ruled that the district had properly developed an IEP "based upon an accepted, proven methodology for facilitating the early primary education of profoundly hearing-impaired children."

Additional Methodology Cases Concerning Children with Hearing Impairments

A long line of cases involving disputes over instructional methodologies for children with hearing impairments reinforces the *Lachman* court's reasoning as the lodestar for guiding courts on this issue. They also are worth mentioning here because the disputes bear some notable resemblances to those at the heart of many autism spectrum disorder methodology cases, particularly in terms of the intensity sometimes displayed by adherents to and advocates of certain methodologies who believe that their preferred methods offer the best approach for children with such disorders.

- C.M. began receiving auditory-verbal therapy (AVT) when she was nine months old. Her parents carefully researched the method before choosing to use it. The Miami-Dade County Early Intervention program paid for one weekly hour of AVT until C.M. turned 3. The district completed its evaluation of C.M. a few days after her third birthday and drafted an IEP recommending that she be placed in a special education class using the verbotonal (VT) approach. Her parents repeatedly asked that the district provide AVT during multiple IEP team and mediation meetings. They filed suit because the district refused to provide AVT. After a lengthy legal battle, the case was decided by the 11th Circuit Court of Appeals. The court determined that the district had appropriately chosen a "recognized and well-established" method. Citing *Lachman*, the court concluded that "[t]he dispute in this case boils down to the parents' belief that AVT is the program best suited to provide C.M. with a quality education. However, under the IDEA there is no entitlement to the 'best' program." (*M.M. ex rel. C.M. v. School Bd. of Miami-Dade County, Fla.*, 45 IDELR 1, 437 F.3d 1085, 1102 (11th Cir. 2006).)

- When the Logues discovered the Central Institute for the Deaf (CID), they decided that their son, Noah, would benefit from the oral communication method this private school offered. Despite the fact that Noah had made progress in a district program using the total communication method, they asked the district to place him at the CID at public expense. The Logues requested a due process hearing after two IEP team meetings failed to result in an agreement. They appealed the resulting decisions against them to the level of the 10th Circuit Court of Appeals. That court cited *Lachman* in concluding in an unpublished opinion "that the IEP was calculated to provide educational benefit to Noah." (*Logue v. Unified Sch. Dist. No. 512*, 28 IDELR 609, 153 F.3d 727 (Table), 5 (10th Cir. 1998).)

- In *Petersen v. Hastings Public Schools*, 21 IDELR 377, 31 F.3d 705 (8th Cir. 1994), a group of parents requested that the district adhere to strict implementation of the Signing Exact English (SEE-II) method. They were unhappy that the district had modified the method by adding "several simplifications of the strict system, which the school district used to allow young students just beginning to sign to learn the language more easily." However, the parents were unable to convince a state hearing officer, a district court, or the 8th Circuit Court of Appeals to order the district to change its chosen methodology. The 8th Circuit wrote:

  > Despite the good intentions of the parents, the Act's requirements do not entitle them to compel the school district to provide their hearing-impaired children with a specific system of signing. The Act "does not require states to provide each [disabled] child with the best possible education at public expense."

- Aaron Cyrex's mother wanted him to attend a private Catholic High School and continue to receive the support of a cued speech interpreter paid for by the school district. The court, however, ruled that because the district's program offered a FAPE, it was not obliged to provide services at the private school. Noting that the facts and legal issues were the same as *Cefalu v. East Baton Rouge Parish School Board*, 103 LRP 33128 (5th Cir. 1997), the lower court in *Cyrex v. Ascension Parish School Board*, 31 IDELR 54, 189 F.3d 467 (5th Cir. 1999) quoted the *Cefalu* case as follows:

  > We therefore hold unambiguously that *the defendants were not legally obligated to provide an on-site sign language interpreter to the plaintiff at the private school.* The plaintiff was offered an individualized education program (IEP) at the public schools, which all parties agreed was appropriate until the plaintiff transferred from the public school where the services were to be provided to the private school he now attends. *Having offered to the plaintiff a free appropriate public education, the local educational agency was not required to provide the on-site interpreter to the plaintiff.* (Emphasis in the original.)

Many of the methodology disputes involving children with hearing impairments were "single issue" cases. That is, the parents were challenging the district's choice of methodology — not, for example, the identification or evaluation of the child, the goals and objectives, the length of the school day, the provision of extended school year services (ESY), or the provision of related services. These cases illustrate how, when methodology stands alone as a discrete issue, school districts are likely to win methodology disputes. In contrast, the autism spectrum disorder methodology disputes often are embedded within challenges to the district's overall program, or to key aspects of that program. That is, parents in these disputes are more likely to challenge the district's methodology for a child with an autism spectrum disorder as part of a broader challenge to the district's goals and objectives or related services for the student, or other aspects of the IEP. That is because the complex nature of autism spectrum disorders and their wide-ranging effects on children have implications for multiple-programming areas. Furthermore, it is the existence of flaws within a district's overall program that often leads hearing officers and courts to reject the district's methodology choices.

In the highly charged atmosphere surrounding autism spectrum disorder methodology disputes, school districts can maximize the educational soundness and legal defensibility of their methodology choices by engaging in sound, broad-based program development at both the global level and the individualized level. Chapter 2 guides school districts through the foundational step of understanding the nature of autism.

ENDNOTES

[1] *Ridgewood Bd. of Educ. v. N.E. for M.E.*, 30 IDELR 41, 172 F.3d 238, 247 (3d Cir. 1999), quoting *Rowley* (internal citations omitted).

[2] *Polk v. Central Susquehanna Intermediate Unit 16*, 441 IDELR 130 (EHLR 441:130), 853 F.2d 171, 184 (3d Cir. 1988).

[3] *Oberti v. Board of Educ. of Borough of Clementon Sch.*, 19 IDELR 908, 995 F.2d 1204, 1213 (3d Cir. 1993) (citation and footnote omitted); *see also Carter v. Florence County Sch. Dist. Four*, 18 IDELR 350, 950 F.2d 156, 160 (4th Cir. 1991).

[4] *Deal ex. rel. Deal v. Hamilton County Bd. of Educ.*, 42 IDELR 109, 392 F.3d 840, 862 (6th Cir. 2004), *cert. denied*, 546 U.S. 936 (2005), adopting 3d Circuit standard.

[5] *Rowley*, 458 U.S. at 192.

[6] *See Gill v. Columbia 93 Sch. Dist.*, 32 IDELR 254, 217 F.3d 1027, 1035 (8th Cir. 2000), citing *Rowley*.

[7] *Burilovich v. Board of Educ. of Lincoln Consol. Schs.*, 32 IDELR 85, 208 F.3d 560, 572 (6th Cir. 2000), *cert. denied*, 531 U.S. 957 (2000), quoting *Rowley*.

[8] *County Sch. Bd. of Henrico County, Va. v. Z.P.*, 45 IDELR 96, 399 F.3d 298, 308 (4th Cir. 2005), quoting *Rowley* (internal citations omitted).

Chapter 2

The Nature of Autism

Before designing and developing a program for children with autism spectrum disorders, school districts must have a solid understanding of the nature of autism including:

- the full spectrum of disorders;

- the ways in which children within the spectrum may qualify for special education services under the IDEA;

- the wide range of educational challenges these children may present due to the heterogeneity of the disorders; and

- the importance of early identification of these children.

As the cases illustrate, this understanding is foundational to a legally defensible program.

Understanding Autism Spectrum Disorders

Increasingly, the literature emphasizes that autism is not a single, homogeneous disorder, but instead it comprises a spectrum of disorders. Although the literature commonly refers to the spectrum of disorders as "autism spectrum disorders," the *Diagnostic and Statistical Manual of Mental Disorders*, Fourth Edition Text Revision (*DSM-IV-TR*), categorizes the spectrum of disorders as Pervasive Developmental Disorders, which include Autistic Disorder, Rett's Disorder, Childhood Disintegrative Disorder, Asperger's Disorder, and Pervasive Developmental Disorder Not Otherwise Specified.[1]

When developing and designing a program for children with autism, school districts need to have an understanding of the full spectrum of disorders and how they may present themselves in the school setting. The National Research Council describes autism as follows:

> Autism is a disorder that is present from birth or very early in development that affects essential human behaviors such as social interaction, the ability to communicate ideas and feelings, imagination, and the establishment of relationships with others. It generally has life-long effects on how children learn to be social beings, to take care of themselves, and to participate in the community. Autism is a developmental disorder of neurobiological origin that is defined on the basis of behavioral and developmental features.
>
> . . . Autism is best characterized as a spectrum of disorders that vary in severity of symptoms, age of onset, and associations with other disorders (e.g., mental retardation, specific language delay, epilepsy). The manifestations of autism vary considerably across children and within an individual child over time. There is no single behavior that is always typical of autism and no behavior that would automatically exclude an individual child from a diagnosis of autism, even though there are strong and consistent commonalities, especially in social deficits.[2]

A 2004 report disseminated by the U.S. Government Accountability Office (GAO) describes the varied nature of the spectrum of disorders and how these disorders manifest in children:

Autism spectrum disorders (ASD) are complex and include a number of disorders. [The report identifies ASDs to include Asperger's disorder, Childhood disintegrative disorder, Rett's disorder, Pervasive developmental disorder — not otherwise specified (PDD-NOS), and Autistic disorder].[3]

Children with ASD may demonstrate a variety of manifestations of the disorder and need services accordingly. For example:

- A child with autistic disorder may have great difficulty communicating and may need services focused on speech development.

- A child with Asperger's disorder may be more verbal than other children with autism and may have average or above-average intelligence, yet still be in need of services.

In addition, services required for an individual child with autism can change over time.[4]

A 2007 clinical report published by the American Academy of Pediatrics states that "[o]ne of the most challenging aspects in recognizing ASDs is the wide heterogeneity of features in individual children."[5]

Unless specifically discussing one of the disorders within the spectrum or a particular disability category under the IDEA, this book will use the term "autism spectrum disorders" to address the population that is the focus of this book. The term "autism spectrum disorders" is a term that is widely used throughout the current literature, and emphasizes the heterogeneous nature of the condition affecting children who fall within the spectrum.

Qualifying for Services under the IDEA

When a child is diagnosed with an autism spectrum disorder, it does not automatically mean that the child qualifies for special education services under the IDEA. To qualify for these services, the child must be evaluated in accordance with the IDEA and determined to have one of the enumerated disabilities under the Act, and also, by reason of the disability, determined to need special education and related services. Autism is one of the enumerated disabilities. *See* 34 CFR 300.8(a)(1). The federal regulations implementing the IDEA define autism to mean:

> a developmental disability significantly affecting verbal and nonverbal communication and social interaction, generally evident before age three, that adversely affects a child's educational performance. Other characteristics often associated with autism are engagement in repetitive activities and stereotyped movements, resistance to environmental change or change in daily routines, and unusual responses to sensory experiences.

34 CFR 300.8(c)(1)(i).

As part of a state's duty to locate, identify, and evaluate all children with disabilities in the state, each state is required to develop criteria for identifying children with disabilities consistent with the IDEA. (*See* 20 USC 1412(a)(3); *see also* U.S. Department of Education discussion of the regulations, 71 Fed. Reg. 46,649 (2006).) Local school districts are required to follow state criteria. The IDEA does not specifically require a diagnosis under the *DSM-IV-TR* for a child to be classified as a child with a disability. However, some states have incorporated the *DSM* criteria as part of the state's criteria for certain disability categories. Additionally, some states have expressly included the specific disorders within the spectrum, including Asperger's Disorder, as part of the IDEA disability category of autism.

Where a state has not included a particular autism spectrum disorder as part of the IDEA disability category of autism, the U.S. Department of Education Office of Special Education Programs (OSEP) has clarified that a child with an autism spectrum disorder such as Asperger's Disorder or Pervasive Developmental Disorder might qualify for services under the IDEA as a child with a disability other than autism, such as Other Health Impaired (OHI) or developmentally delayed:

> [I]f a child with Asperger's Syndrome meets the criteria in the Part B definition of "autism" at [34 CFR 300.8(c)(1)], a child with that condition could be found eligible for services under Part B. Because a child with this condition could be found eligible for services under Part B under one of the existing disability categories, we do not believe it necessary to address the question of whether Asperger's Syndrome should be treated in the same manner as attention deficit disorder and attention deficit hyperactivity disorder, the examples of which were added to the "other health impairment" definition at [34 CFR 300.8(c)(9)]. The conditions listed in the Part B definition of "other health impairment" are examples of conditions that could render a child eligible under that category. Regardless of whether Asperger's Syndrome is identified as a condition that could render a child "other health impaired," we do not believe it would be inconsistent with Part B for a State to permit school districts to evaluate children with Asperger's Syndrome to determine whether they could be considered other health impaired. In addition, children with Asperger's Syndrome aged 3 through 9 can be classified as developmentally delayed if the State and LEA utilize that classification, and if the child's condition meets the criteria in the definition of developmental delay adopted by the State. (*Letter to Williams*, 33 IDELR 249 (OSEP 2000).)

> While Part B does not explicitly mention PDD [Pervasive Developmental Disorder], we believe that a child with PDD could be found eligible for services under Part B if, through an appropriate evaluation, the team determines that the child's condition meets one of the disability categories described in [§300.8] of the Part B regulations, including the applicable State diagnostic criteria, and because of that disability, the child needs special education and related services. Some states' diagnostic criteria for autism explicitly recognize that a PDD diagnosis satisfies the definition of autism for Part B purposes. In other instances, a child who does not meet the definition and diagnostic criteria for autism, may meet the definition and diagnostic criteria for another disability category, such as other health impairment.

> In addition, children with PDD ages 3 through 9 can be classified as developmentally delayed if the State and LEA utilize that classification, and if the PDD constitutes a developmental delay under applicable diagnostic criteria. Further, IDEA '97 clarifies that "[n]othing in the Act requires that [children] be classified by their disability so long as each child who has a disability listed in [§300.8] and who, by reason of that disability, needs special education and related service[ ] is regarded as a child with a disability under Part B of the Act." [34 CFR 300.111(d).] (*Letter to Coe*, 32 IDELR 204 (OSEP 1999).)

Given these state differences, unless a particular case otherwise specifies, this book will use the term "autism spectrum disorders" rather than autism even when referring to children who are receiving special education services, since the qualifying disability category may not be that of autism.

Recognizing the Wide Range of Symptomatology and Degrees of Impairment

The case of *County School Board of Henrico County, VA v. R.T.*, 45 IDELR 274, 433 F. Supp. 2d 657 (E.D. Va. 2006), illustrates the complexity of the disorder and the resulting educational challenges. RT's parents noticed that he was developmentally delayed when he was less than 1 year old, at which point he began receiving speech and occupational therapy (OT) services under an Individualized Family Services Plan (IFSP) developed by a local parent-infant program. About one year later, in October 1999, he was diagnosed by a pediatric neurologist as having autism and language delays. He was thereafter identified as needing special education services by Henrico County Public Schools in spring 2000, and he began receiving homebound speech and OT services under an Individualized Education Program (IEP).

RT entered the school district's preschool for developmentally delayed children (PEDD) in fall 2001, which implemented both group and individualized educational strategies. Midway through the 2001-2002 school year, RT's mother became concerned about what she considered to be RT's lack of sufficient progress toward meeting his IEP goals. She requested that RT be admitted to the district's autism program at Twin Hickory Public Elementary School for 2002-2003, and at the same time began researching applied behavioral analysis (ABA) methodology on her own. She and another individual designed and implemented a home-based program of ABA methodology for RT during the summer of 2002, and RT's mother was pleased with the progress her child made.

The IEP developed in September 2002, when RT began attending Twin Hickory, was largely the same as his April 2002 IEP. RT's mother requested that ABA methodology be included in this IEP rather than the TEACCH methodology used at Twin Hickory, and she presented as support both her research on ABA and input about the progress RT had made that summer using ABA. The district considered but denied this request, and the IEP reflected that RT's existing goals would continue under the TEACCH methodology until a reevaluation could be conducted. Because of their ongoing concerns about the school district's services for RT, his parents began the process of applying for his enrollment at a private school that used ABA methodology even as the school year at Twin Hickory got under way.

During fall 2002, the district and the parents conducted evaluations of RT, the results of which indicated that in addition to having autism, he was significantly cognitively impaired (although his age and lack of communication skills made it impossible to accurately gauge the extent of his impairment). During this period, RT's IEP team met twice more (on October 30 and on November 4). After the October 30 meeting, at which RT's mother presented a letter from a specialist stating that reversal of RT's autistic symptoms had occurred using ABA methodology, the district drafted a new IEP, which was then discussed on November 4. That IEP contained 24 goals, 17 of which were the same as the goals in the April 2002 and September 2002 IEPs. Frustrated and convinced that RT's lack of progress on these goals was due to the district's continued use of an inappropriate methodology for him, the parents withdrew RT from Twin Hickory and enrolled him at the private school and requested a due process hearing seeking reimbursement for the cost of RT's private school.

The hearing officer held that the district had denied RT a FAPE, based in large part on evidence that RT quickly made "exceptional gains" and "flourished" at the private school. The school district appealed that decision. The district court that heard the appeal also ruled in favor of the parents, and issued a Memorandum Opinion, which provides pertinent explanation regarding the nature of autism:

> Often called Autism Spectrum Disorder, "[a]utism is a syndrome — a collection of symptoms, with different children experiencing distinct symptoms with varying degrees of impairment from their symptoms." . . . "The main characteristics that differentiate autism from other developmental disorders include 'behavioral deficits in

eye contact, orienting to one's name, joint attention behaviors (e.g., pointing, show-ing), pretend play, imitation, nonverbal communication, and language development.'" Many autistic children appear to have tuned the world out and are in their own worlds, not paying attention to others or engaging in normal social interactions. . . .

Testimony by several experts during the administrative hearing explained that autistic children like RT lack two skills that are essential to learning. First such children lack so-called "imitation" skills, which are the ability to watch another do an action and imitate that action. Much of what a young child learns to do, especially a child who lacks expressive or receptive language skills, is through imitation.

Second, many autistic children lack so-called "joint attention" skills, which are the ability to focus attention on something that is pointed out to the child by another. . . . More profoundly, autistic students with significant deficiencies in basic attention skills, known as "attending skills," cannot maintain focus on a task for even a few seconds. . . . [W]ithout attending skills, a child cannot maintain attention long enough to learn.

The district court ultimately agreed with the hearing officer's conclusion, holding that RT's dra-matic improvement at the private school helped demonstrate that the district had grossly miscalculated his cognitive abilities and, as a result, provided him with inappropriate IEPs and inadequate services, thus denying him a FAPE. This case demonstrates some of the challenges school districts face. Children with autism spectrum disorders exhibit a wide range of abilities and limitations. The abilities of a child with an autism spectrum disorder can be hidden by the child's limitations. Multidisciplinary teams should be prepared to evaluate children whose abilities may fall within a wide range and not be readily apparent. Broad-based program planning should contemplate these differences.

Cognitive Impairments

Some children with autism disorders have cognitive impairments, including severe cognitive im-pairments.

According to the *DSM-IV-TR*, for children with Autistic Disorder, "[i]n most cases, there is an associated diagnosis of Mental Retardation, which can range from mild to profound. There may be abnormalities in the development of cognitive skills."[6]

The case of *J.P. ex rel. Popson v. West Clark Community Schools*, 38 IDELR 5, 230 F. Supp. 2d 910 (S.D. Ind. 2002), illustrates the educational challenges for a child with autism and severe cognitive impairments. J.P. was diagnosed with autism when he was 2 years old (and with speech apraxia some-time thereafter). He was provided with special education services in the county's First Steps program, including physical therapy until age 3, at which time he enrolled in a public preschool. The district evaluated J.P. at the time of his enrollment and determined that he was "severely autistic" based on findings that he

(a) displayed "a marked impairment in the use of multiple nonverbal behaviors;" (b) had not yet developed peer relationships appropriate to his developmental level; (c) lacked verbal communication; (d) did not engage in spontaneous imaginative play; and (e) exhibited stereotyped repetitive motor mechanisms.

As discussed later in more detail, following the development of J.P.'s IEP and his enrollment in a public preschool program from January 2000 through summer 2000, a methodology dispute began to emerge between J.P.'s parents and the school district. The parents requested a due process hearing to challenge the district's IEP and services, which resulted in a decision in the district's favor. Subsequent appeals by the parents to both the Board of Special Education Appeal and district court also were concluded in the district's favor.

Average to Above-Average Cognitive Abilities

In contrast, some children with autism spectrum disorders have average to above-average cognitive abilities. One of the features that distinguishes Asperger's Disorder from some other autism spectrum disorders is that "there are no clinically significant delays in cognitive development as manifested by expressing normal curiosity about the environment or in the acquisition of age-appropriate learning skills and adaptive behaviors (other than in social interaction). . . ."[7] Nevertheless, these children often present other types of significant educational challenges.

The case of *Mr. I. ex rel. L.I. v. Maine School Administrative District No. 55*, 47 IDELR 121, 480 F.3d 1 (1st Cir. 2007), illustrates the kind of educational challenges a child with Asperger's Disorder with average to above-average intelligence can present. LI excelled academically in elementary school, but started demonstrating problems with peer relationships as well as sadness and anxiety in fourth and fifth grade. Her grades also declined from "high honors" to "honors" in fifth grade. After some improvement in her peer relationships toward the end of fifth grade (during which time she also received psychological counseling and prescription anti-depressants), LI experienced even more severe problems with peer interaction at the beginning of her sixth-grade year, and also demonstrated both academic performance difficulties and signs of self-cutting during that time. On October 1 of that year, LI attempted suicide.

Following her suicide attempt, LI was diagnosed with Asperger's Disorder (as well as adjustment disorder with depressed mood). However, the school district determined that her disability did not adversely affect her educational performance, a requirement for eligibility under the IDEA, and the district therefore declined to provide her with special education services. LI's parents challenged this determination through a due process hearing. The hearing officer found for the district, and the parents appealed. The district court reversed and found for the parents, and (on appeal by the school district) the 1st Circuit Court of Appeals affirmed this portion of the decision in the parents' favor.

In describing the effects of LI's Asperger's Disorder, the court noted that despite her undisputed intellectual capability,

> LI "experience[d] significant limitations in many areas of adaptive skills" and executive skills, "which likely contribute[d] to her behavioral and emotional difficulties."

> The court added in a footnote: "Adaptive skills are those necessary to cope with common life demands and meet the standards of personal independence appropriate for one's age, sociocultural background, and community setting. Executive skills are those necessary to think abstractly and to plan, initiate, monitor, and stop complex behavior."

The court also took note of experts' conclusions that "LI had 'poor pragmatic language skills' and 'significant social understanding deficits,'" as well as the lower court's treatment of LI's suicide attempt as

> simply the darkest point in the spectrum of [her] educational difficulties. . . . The signs of LI's Asperger's revealed themselves in the fourth grade, when she began experiencing difficulty with peer relationships, and first translated into a measurable impact on her schoolwork in the fifth and sixth grades, when her grades declined. More importantly, there is every indication that these symptoms will persist, to one degree or another. . . .

According to a clinical report from the American Academy of Pediatrics:

> Even highly functioning students with ASDs often require accommodations and other supports such as provision of explicit directions, modification of classroom and home-

work assignments, organizational supports, access to a computer and word-processing software for writing tasks, and social communication skills training.[8]

Ensuring Early Identification

When examining the nature of autism, it is important to consider that research increasingly supports the notion of a crucial period (sometimes termed a "window of opportunity") for learning that makes early identification and intervention critical for achieving long-term improved outcomes. This research-based concern is emphasized throughout the 2004 GAO Report:[9]

> According to a 2001 National Research Council report, intervention at an early age is a key feature of successful approaches to educating children with autism.

> While no known cure for ASD exists, the general agreement is that early diagnosis followed by appropriate treatment can improve outcomes for later years for most children with ASD.

> NRC reported a general consensus that [several] features were key to the education of children with autism across preschool programs [including] [i]ntervention programs as soon as an autism spectrum disorder is seriously considered.

The 2007 clinical report from the American Academy of Pediatrics further emphasizes this concern:

> In the last two decades, research and program development in the area of educational intervention have focused largely on very young children with ASDs because of earlier identification and *evidence that early intensive intervention may result in substantially better outcomes.*[10] (Emphasis added.)

This research, coupled with the case law, suggests that early identification and intervention should be considered to be key components of an effective program for children with autism spectrum disorders. *Amanda J. ex rel. Annette J. v. Clark County School District*, 103 LRP 33278, 267 F.3d 877 (9th Cir. 2001), is one case that emphasizes the importance of early identification and intervention.

When Amanda was 2 years old, a child psychologist who evaluated her found that she had deficits in communication and daily living skills and recommended that she be placed in the school district's early childhood program for a determination of her special education eligibility. The district subsequently conducted a psychological evaluation in March 1995, which indicated "mixed" results on the Autism Behavior Checklist, noted below-average social skills and developmental delay, and recommended a special education eligibility assessment, as well as various services to address her behavior and speech/language needs. The report containing this information was not provided to the parents.

The district's speech pathologist also evaluated Amanda in March 1995, and found her to qualify as "severely autistic" under the Childhood Autism Rating Scale. The speech pathologist recommended speech/language therapy, certain further assessments, and various classroom-based activities to address Amanda's speech deficits. However, no documentation existed in the case record to establish that this information was shared with the parents.

In April 1995, Amanda was deemed eligible for special education services as "developmentally delayed" by an eligibility team because of her language, cognitive, self-help and social/emotional difficulties. Amanda's mother requested copies of the child's assessment reports at that point, but did not receive anything until after the initial IEP was completed in May 1995 — and then she received only a two-page summary of the district psychologist's recommendations, which did not mention the reports indicating possible autism.

At the May 1995 initial IEP team meeting, the IEP team addressed Amanda's "delays in language, cognitive, social skills, and self-help." The issue of autism does not appear to have been a factor in the discussion. In fall 1995, Amanda was placed in an early childhood education class taught by a teacher who had "a master's degree in early childhood special education but no special training or experience with autistic children." In October, at the request of Amanda's teacher, the IEP team reconvened to review and revise some of the child's goals in light of her lack of progress in skill development across the areas of concern. The IEP team made changes to Amanda's IEP, again without apparent discussion or consideration of autism as a potential diagnosis.

On or around Oct. 31, 1995, Amanda and her family moved to California, whereupon Amanda's mother authorized the transfer of the child's files from the Siegle Diagnostic Center in Nevada to her new California preschool. In December 1995, Amanda's uncle (a doctor) referred her for an evaluation due to characteristics suggesting autism, resulting in an affirmative diagnosis of autism in January 1996 (confirmed in February through a second opinion). A separate evaluation by American River Speech and Hearing Associates in February yielded a diagnosis of severe language delay, but not autism.

At an April 1996 IEP team meeting, Amanda's parents were given for the first time copies of the Clark County school district's 1995 reports indicating the district's detection of possible autism more than a year earlier. In October 1997, they requested a due process hearing to determine whether the Nevada school district had misidentified Amanda as developmentally delayed and, thereby, failed to provide her with a FAPE. The hearing officer decided in favor of the parents; on appeal, however, a state review officer (who did not address the procedural violations found by the hearing officer) reversed that decision. The parents then appealed the SRO's ruling in federal court. When the district court affirmed the SRO's decision, they appealed to the 9th Circuit Court of Appeals.

The 9th Circuit came down squarely in favor of the parents, holding that the district's "egregious" procedural violation of failing to give the parents copies of Amanda's initial evaluation reports resulted in a denial of FAPE. In explaining its decision, the court stated:

> This is a situation where the District had information in its records which, if disclosed, would have changed the educational approach used for Amanda. . . . This is a particularly troubling violation, where, as here, the parents had no other source of information available to them. No one will ever know the extent to which this failure to act upon early detection of the possibility of autism has seriously impaired Amanda's ability to fully develop the skills to receive education and to fully participate as a member of the community.
>
> . . . Autism is a developmental disorder; those affected by autism exhibit significant deficiencies in communication skills, social interaction and motor control. Early intervention can lead to positive outcomes, particularly when children are placed in highly structured, specialized, and individualized programs.
>
> . . . [The district's] procedural violations, which prevented Amanda's parents from learning critical medical information about their child, rendered the accomplishment of the IDEA's goals — and the achievement of FAPE — impossible.

The court's remarks shed light on how compelling the "window of opportunity" research and resulting expert opinion can be. The court's remarks further reveal its belief that had the district identified Amanda as a child with autism, it would have materially altered the educational program provided to the child.

After a school district ensures a foundational understanding of autism, including:

✓ the full spectrum of disorders;

✓ the ways in which children within the spectrum may qualify for special education services under the IDEA;

✓ the wide range of educational challenges these children may present due to the heterogeneity of the disorders; and

✓ the importance of early identification of these children,

it can take the next step of broad-based program design and development. Chapter 3 guides school districts through this next step of design and development of a comprehensive program for children with autism spectrum disorders.

ENDNOTES

[1] *See Diagnostic and Statistical Manual of Mental Disorders*, Fourth Edition Text Revision (DSM-IV-TR). Washington, D.C.: American Psychiatric Association. (2000).

[2] National Research Council. (2001). *Educating children with autism*. 11. Committee on Educational Interventions for Children with Autism. Catherine Lord and James P. McGee, eds. Division of Behavioral and Social Sciences and Education. Washington, D.C.: National Academy Press.

[3] U.S. Government Accountability Office. *Special education: Children with autism*, 11. Washington, D.C., January 2005.

[4] *Id* at 23.

[5] Johnson, Chris Plauche, M.D., M.Ed., Myers, Scott M., M.D., & Council on Children with Disabilities. (2007). Identification and evaluation of children with autism spectrum disorders. *Pediatrics,* vol. 120: num. 5: 1190.

[6] *Diagnostic and Statistical Manual of Mental Disorders*, Fourth Edition Text Revision (DSM-IV-TR), 71-72. Washington, D.C.: American Psychiatric Association. (2000).

[7] *Diagnostic and Statistical Manual of Mental Disorders*, Fourth Edition Text Revision (DSM-IV-TR), 80. Washington, D.C.: American Psychiatric Association. (2000).

[8] Myers, Scott M., M.D. (2007). Management of children with autism spectrum disorders. *Pediatrics,* vol. 120: num. 5: 1167.

[9] U.S. Government Accountability Office. *Special education: Children with autism*, 10, 13, 34. Washington, D.C., January 2005.

[10] Myers, Scott M., M.D. (2007). Management of children with autism spectrum disorders. *Pediatrics,* vol. 120: num. 5: 1163.

Chapter 3

Design and Development of a Comprehensive Program

With a foundational understanding of autism spectrum disorders in place, school districts can begin designing and developing a comprehensive program for children with these disorders. This process ideally should take place separately from the IEP process, so that individual programming can occur within a sound, existing framework. While much of the litigation involving children with autism spectrum disorders is characterized as a dispute over methodology, the cases reveal that a school district's legal vulnerability often stems from holes in the child's overall program.

While the methodology wars rage on, consensus regarding the essential components of a program for children with autism spectrum disorders is emerging. Therefore, before diving into the methodology debate, school districts should focus on building a comprehensive program for children with these disorders, one which ensures the capacity to individualize within the program.

Identifying the Components of a Comprehensive Program

According to the 2001 National Research Council report, "a consensus [is visible] across programs on the factors that result in program effectiveness."[1] The report cites such factors as early intervention; an intensive number of hours (20-45 hours per week); active family involvement; highly trained, specialized staff; ongoing objective assessment of a child's progress; and systematic teaching to address a range of needs.

This general sentiment is echoed in a 2007 clinical report from the American Academy of Pediatrics in its discussion of early childhood intervention programs for children with autism spectrum disorders:

Although programs may differ in philosophy and relative emphasis on particular strategies, they share many common goals, and there is a growing consensus that important principles and components of effective early childhood intervention for children with ASDs include the following:

- entry into intervention as soon as an ASD diagnosis is seriously considered rather than deferring until a definitive diagnosis is made;

- provision of intensive intervention, with active engagement of the child at least 25 hours per week, 12 months per year, in systematically planned, developmentally appropriate educational activities designed to address identified objectives;

- low student-to-teacher ratio to allow sufficient amounts of 1-on-1 time and small-group instruction to meet specific individualized goals;

- inclusion of a family component (including parent training as indicated);

- promotion of opportunities for interaction with typically developing peers to the extent that these opportunities are helpful in addressing specified educational goals;

- ongoing measurement and documentation of the individual child's progress toward educational objectives, resulting in adjustments in programming when indicated;

- incorporation of a high degree of structure through elements such as predictable routine, visual activity schedules, and clear physical boundaries to minimize distractions;

- implementation of strategies to apply learned skills to new environments and situations (generalization) and to maintain functional use of these skills; and

- use of assessment-based curricula that address:

  - functional, spontaneous communication;

  - social skills, including joint attention, imitation, reciprocal interaction, initiation, and self-management;

  - functional adaptive skills that prepare the child for increased responsibility and independence;

  - reduction of disruptive or maladaptive behavior by using empirically supported strategies, including functional assessment;

  - cognitive skills, such as symbolic play and perspective taking; and

  - traditional readiness skills and academic skills as developmentally indicated.[2]

When designing and developing a program for children with autism spectrum disorders, school districts should take into account the scope and complexity of the spectrum of disorders and the resulting program features necessary for the provision of a FAPE:

Educational interventions, including behavioral strategies and habilitative therapies, are the cornerstones of management of ASDs. These interventions address communication, social skills, daily-living skills, play and leisure skills, academic achievement, and maladaptive behaviors.[3]

The program must be able to address both the academic and nonacademic needs of such children:

Education [of children with autism] covers a wide range "of skills or knowledge — including not only academic learning, but also socialization, adaptive skills, language and communication, and reduction of behavior problems — to assist a child to develop independence and personal responsibility."[4]

Educational objectives for children with autism should include the development of:

- social skills;

- expressive verbal language, receptive language, nonverbal communications skills;

- a functional symbolic communication system;

- engagement and flexibility in developmentally appropriate tasks and play;

- fine and gross motor skills;

- cognitive skills (symbolic play and academic skills);

- conventional/appropriate behaviors; and

- independent organizational skills and skills for success in a regular classroom.[5]

Given the potential impact of autism spectrum disorders on a wide range of areas related to educational performance, a district's ability to provide a FAPE to even one child with autism depends on its readiness to provide a variety of services. According to the Special Education Expenditure Project (SEEP), expenditures for special education services for children with autism spectrum disorders can be categorized as follows:

- special education classes — classes designed specifically for students with disabilities, taught by special education teachers;

- resource specialists — includ[ing] special education teachers who either pull students with disabilities out of regular education classes or go into regular education classrooms to work with students with disabilities;

- related services — school psychologists, social workers, school nurses, speech/language specialists and physical/occupational and other therapists; and

- other special education services — community-based training, extended time services, and summer school.[6]

It is important to note that none of these key program elements are tied to a particular methodology. The design and development of a comprehensive program assures a context in which FAPE can be provided and demonstrated regardless of the chosen methodology.

The Role of the State

What is the role of the state department of education when designing and developing a comprehensive program? According to the U.S. Supreme Court in *Rowley*:

> The Act expressly charges States with the responsibility of "acquiring and disseminating to teachers and administrators of programs for handicapped children significant information derived from educational research, demonstration, and similar projects, and [of] adopting, where appropriate, promising educational practices and materials." §1413(a)(3). In the face of such a clear statutory directive, it seems highly unlikely that Congress intended courts to overturn a State's choice of appropriate educational theories in a proceeding conducted pursuant to 20 USC 1415(e)(2).[7]

The language of the Act has been strengthened since it was quoted by the Court in *Rowley*. When reauthorizing the IDEA in 2004, Congress incorporated the objectives of the federal Elementary and Secondary Education Act (ESEA) (as amended by the No Child Left Behind Act (NCLB)) in authorizing states to use IDEA funds

> [t]o provide technical assistance to schools and local educational agencies, and direct services . . . including providing professional development to special and regular edu-

cation teachers, who teach children with disabilities, *based on scientifically based research* to improve educational instruction, in order to improve academic achievement to meet or exceed the objectives established by the State under section 6311(b)(2)(G) of [the Elementary and Secondary Education Act of 1965].

20 USC 1411(e)(2)(C)(xi) (emphasis added).

States must establish policies for implementing the IDEA. The IDEA 2004 sets forth state eligibility requirements which are described in the regulations as follows:

> A State is eligible for assistance under Part B of the Act for a fiscal year if the State submits a plan that provides assurances to the Secretary that the State has in effect policies and procedures to ensure that the State meets the conditions in §§ 300.101 through 300.176.

34 CFR 300.100.

Additionally, it is the role of the state, with the assistance of an advisory panel, to provide guidance:

> The State must establish and maintain an advisory panel for the purpose of providing policy guidance with respect to special education and related services for children with disabilities in the State.

34 CFR 300.167.

School districts must comply with the policies established by the state:

> The LEA, in providing for the education of children with disabilities within its jurisdiction, must have in effect policies, procedures, and programs that are consistent with the State policies and procedures established under §§ 300.101 through 300.163, and §§ 300.165 through 300.174.

34 CFR 300.201.

States may set higher standards than those established in federal law. However, when states adopt standards that exceed federal standards, they are required to provide clear notice to school districts:

> *Rulemaking.* Each State that receives funds under Part B of the Act must —
>
> (1) Ensure that any State rules, regulations, and policies relating to this part conform to the purposes of this part;
>
> (2) Identify in writing to LEAs located in the State and the Secretary any such rule, regulation, or policy as a State imposed requirement that is not required by Part B of the Act and Federal regulations; and
>
> (3) Minimize the number of rules, regulations, and policies to which the LEAs and schools located in the State are subject under Part B of the Act.

34 CFR 300.199(a).

The state is responsible for ensuring that teachers are highly qualified through such means as providing professional development. In its discussion of the final IDEA 2004 regulations, the USDE stated:

[T]he clear intent of the Act is to ensure that all children with disabilities have teachers with the subject matter knowledge and teaching skills necessary to assist children with disabilities to achieve to high academic standards.

. . .

To help States and districts meet these standards, section 651 of the Act authorizes State Personnel Development grants to help States reform and improve their systems for personnel preparation and professional development in early intervention, educational, and transition services in order to improve results for children with disabilities. In addition, section 662 of the Act authorizes funding for institutions of higher education, LEAs, and other eligible local entities to improve or develop new training programs for teachers and other personnel serving children with disabilities.

71 Fed. Reg. 46,555 (2006).

With regard to alternative teacher certification programs, the USDE states in its discussion of the final IDEA regulations:

The individual also must receive, before and while teaching, high-quality professional development that is sustained, intensive, and classroom-focused and have intensive supervision that consists of structured guidance and regular ongoing support.

71 Fed. Reg. 46,557 (2006); *see also* 34 CFR 300.18(b)(2)(i)(A)-(B).

In many programs for children with autism spectrum disorders, including in privately run home-based programs and private school programs, paraprofessionals are relied upon to implement certain methodologies. The extent to which public schools can utilize paraprofessionals to implement certain methodologies depends on the state. It is the role of the state to determine the appropriate use of a paraprofessional:

The qualifications under paragraph (a) of this section [which states must establish] must include qualifications for . . . paraprofessionals that . . . [a]llow paraprofessionals and assistants who are appropriately trained and supervised, in accordance with State law, regulation, or written policy, in meeting the requirements of this part to be used to assist in the provision of special education and related services under this part to children with disabilities.

34 CFR 300.156(b)(2)(iii).

The USDE in its discussion of the final IDEA 2004 regulations states:

The Act makes clear that the use of paraprofessionals and assistants who are appropriately trained and supervised must be contingent on State law, regulation, and written policy giving States the option of determining whether paraprofessionals and assistants can be used to assist in the provision of special education and related services under Part B of the Act, and, if so, to what extent their use would be permissible. However, it is critical that States that use paraprofessionals and assistants to assist in providing special education and related services to children with disabilities do so in a manner that is consistent with the rights of children with disabilities to FAPE under Part B of the Act. There is no need to provide additional guidance on how States and LEAs should use paraprofessionals and assistants because States have the flexibility to determine whether to use them, and, if so, to determine the scope of their responsibilities.

71 Fed. Reg. 46,612 (2006).

States have responded to these obligations in a variety of ways. In one notable example, the Texas Education Agency requires IEP teams in Texas to consider the use of an array of strategies when developing an IEP for an identified child with autism in that state. The regulation provides as follows:

For students [with autism], the strategies described in paragraphs (1)-(11) of this subsection shall be considered, based on peer-reviewed, research-based educational programming practices to the extent practicable and, when needed, addressed in the IEP:

(1) extended educational programming (for example: extended day and/or extended school year services that consider the duration of programs/settings based on assessment of behavior, social skills, communication, academics, and self-help skills);

(2) daily schedules reflecting minimal unstructured time and active engagement in learning activities (for example: lunch, snack, and recess periods that provide flexibility within routines; adapt to individual skill levels; and assist with schedule changes, such as changes involving substitute teachers and pep rallies);

(3) in-home and community-based training or viable alternatives that assist the student with acquisition of social/behavioral skills (for example: strategies that facilitate maintenance and generalization of such skills from home to school, school to home, home to community, and school to community);

(4) positive behavior support strategies based on relevant information, for example:

(A) antecedent manipulation, replacement behaviors, reinforcement strategies, and data-based decisions; and

(B) a Behavior Intervention Plan developed from a Functional Behavioral Assessment that uses current data related to target behaviors and addresses behavioral programming across home, school, and community-based settings;

(5) beginning at any age, consistent with subsections (g) of this section, futures planning for integrated living, work, community, and educational environments that considers skills necessary to function in current and post-secondary environments;

(6) parent/family training and support, provided by qualified personnel with experience in Autism Spectrum Disorders (ASD), that, for example:

(A) provides a family with skills necessary for a child to succeed in the home/community setting;

(B) includes information regarding resources (for example: parent support groups, workshops, videos, conferences, and materials designed to increase parent knowledge of specific teaching/management techniques related to the child's curriculum); and

(C) facilitates parental carryover of in-home training (for example: strategies for behavior management and developing structured home environments and/or communication training so that parents are active participants in promoting the continuity of interventions across all settings);

(7) suitable staff-to-student ratio appropriate to identified activities and as needed to achieve social/behavioral progress based on the child's developmental and learning level (acquisition, fluency, maintenance, generalization) that encourages work towards individual independence as determined by, for example:

(A) adaptive behavior evaluation results;

(B) behavioral accommodation needs across settings; and

(C) transitions within the school day;

(8) communication interventions, including language forms and functions that enhance effective communication across settings (for example: augmentative, incidental, and naturalistic teaching);

(9) social skills supports and strategies based on social skills assessment/curriculum and provided across settings (for example: trained peer facilitators (e.g., circle of friends), video modeling, social stories, and role playing);

(10) professional educator/staff support (for example: training provided to personnel who work with the student to assure the correct implementation of techniques and strategies described in the IEP); and

(11) teaching strategies based on peer-reviewed, research-based practices for students with ASD (for example: those associated with discrete-trial training, visual supports, applied behavior analysis, structured learning, augmentative communication, or social skills training).

19 Tex. Admin. Code §89.1055(e).

School districts should incorporate in their program design any state requirements, since districts must comply with the regulatory requirements of the state. School districts are entitled to look to their respective state educational agencies for the guidance and support mandated by the IDEA. School districts should rely upon and follow the policy guidance of the state since hearing officers and courts must give deference to such guidance.

Ensure Relevant District Personnel Have Appropriate Training, Expertise

Program design and development should include an assessment of the personnel development needs of the staff and the provision of ongoing personnel development. One of the conditions of local educational agency (LEA) eligibility for IDEA funds is that school districts ensure proper personnel development. The IDEA 2004 regulations state:

The LEA must ensure that all personnel necessary to carry out Part B of the Act are appropriately and adequately prepared, subject to the requirements of § 300.156 (related to personnel qualifications) and section 2122 of the ESEA.

34 CFR 300.207.

The U.S. Department of Education, in its discussion of the final IDEA 2004 regulations, stated:

We believe the regulations already address the commenters' concern and reflect the Department's position that high-quality professional development, including the use of scientifically based instructional practices, is important to ensure that personnel have the skills and knowledge necessary to improve the academic achievement and functional performance of children with disabilities.

71 Fed. Reg. 46,625 (2006).

Careful attention should be paid to the training and expertise necessary to execute the district's broad-based program for children with autism spectrum disorders, including the various methodologies the program might employ. Ensuring that relevant staff members are adequately trained and qualified to implement the district's program is an essential step, both from an educational perspective and a legal one.

The case law on this point is clear: the legal defensibility of a given program including methodologies will depend in large part on the extent to which relevant district personnel are trained and qualified to implement it. For example, in the *Popson* case mentioned earlier, the district court looked with favor upon the fact that

J.P.'s teachers clearly were familiar with the special problems and needs of autistic children. Special education supervisor Reich testified that she had gone to many conferences and workshops on autism. Speech therapist Wahl testified that she was specifically trained in the ABA/DTT techniques which the Popsons advocate and that she uses them in almost everything she does.[8]

Another case, *Deal ex. rel. Deal v. Hamilton County Board of Education*, 42 IDELR 109, 392 F.3d 840, 847 (6th Cir. 2004), *cert. denied*, 546 U.S. 936 (2005), and the related case of *Deal v. Hamilton County Department of Education*, 46 IDELR 45 (E.D. Tenn. 2006), *aff'd*, 108 LRP 1858 (6th Cir. 2008), also illustrate the importance of appropriate professional development. In that dispute, the Hamilton County Board of Education and Zachary's parents, Mr. and Mrs. Deal, developed the child's first IEP for him in 1997, when he was 3 years old. At the same time that Zachary began attending a preschool comprehensive development class (CDC) in the district, as called for by his IEP, the Deals began to teach their son at home using a program of Applied Behavioral Analysis (ABA) methodology developed by the Center for Autism and Related Disorders (CARD).

At a May 1998 IEP team meeting to discuss ESY services, the Deals requested that the district fund their 40-hour per week home-based program of ABA methodology and year-round speech therapy, which the district rejected in favor of ESY services consisting of three 45-minute speech therapy sessions per week. The district also refused to provide data to the Deals regarding the effectiveness of its program.

Zachary's October 1998 IEP was 95 pages long. It called for 35 hours per week of special education plus related services, such as physical therapy and speech therapy, and included many annual goals. The Deals continued to request funding for a private home-based program consisting of ABA methodology instead. IEP team meetings were held in November and December of 1998 as well as in February, March and May of 1999; meanwhile, Zachary attended school only 16 percent of the time that school year.

At the May 1999 IEP team meeting, the Deals requested an ESY program consisting of 43 hours per week of one-on-one ABA methodology and five hours per week of speech therapy, but the IEP team declined to offer ESY at all after determining that Zachary's lack of attendance that year prevented them from being able to document the regression that he might suffer without ESY.

Two IEP team meetings were held in August 1999, and the district's proposed IEP offered Zachary continued attendance in CDC; participation in a regular kindergarten class (plus lunch) three times per week for 15 minutes, to increase over time according to his tolerance level; a trained classroom assistant; use of a variety of instructional methodologies (in what was regarded as an "eclectic" approach); and the related services of speech therapy, occupational therapy and physical therapy.

However, the Deals believed Zachary needed more time in a regular education classroom as well as a program consisting of ABA methodology, and in September of 1999 they notified the district that they had enrolled Zachary in a private preschool where he was in regular pre-K for three hours per day, two days per week, with a personal aide funded by the Deals. The Deals requested a due process hearing in September 1999 to challenge HCDE's proposed IEP.

The procedural history of this dispute is long and complex, and different portions of the courts' rulings are discussed where relevant throughout this book. To briefly summarize here: The due process hearing in that case lasted 27 days, and tens of thousands of pages of exhibits were submitted. The administrative law judge (ALJ) decided in favor of the parents on most of the disputed issues. The school district appealed the matter to federal district court, which reversed certain portions of the ALJ's ruling. On subsequent appeal to the 6th Circuit Court of Appeals, the higher court decided the matter in favor of the parents on some issues, but also remanded the matter back to the district court to decide whether the district's proposed IEP was reasonably calculated to provide meaningful educational benefit to Zachary. The district court (on remand) concluded that the school district's IEP was reasonably calculated to provide FAPE, noting with approval the substantial evidence presented regarding the training and expertise of the district's staff:

> Lisa Steele had nine years of experience teaching special education preschool classes at the CDC preschool when [Zachary] joined her class.[9]

> Paula Wiesen, a certified speech and language pathologist, was [Zachary's] preschool teacher for the 1998-1999 school year. Ms. Wiesen had worked with numerous autistic students before working with [Zachary] and had eight years experience in special education.[10]

> Dr. Freeman found that both Ms. Steele and Ms. Wiesen were adequately trained professionals. She testified that Ms. Steele had "extensive training" as a certified special education teacher with a masters in early childhood development, as well as extensive training in ABA techniques.[11]

The district court's determination regarding the appropriateness of the school district's IEP was later affirmed by the 6th Circuit Court of Appeals. (*See Deal ex rel. Deal v. Hamilton County Dep't of Educ.*, 49 IDELR 123 (6th Cir. 2008); *see also Dong v. Board of Educ. of Rochester Community Schs.*, 31 IDELR 157, 197 F.3d 793, 801 (6th Cir. 1999) ("[A]s the district court observed, the school staff members present at the IEP [Team meeting], Lisa's school psychologist, speech pathologist, and teacher, were 'extremely well qualified in the area of autism treatments, and they were fully qualified to determine if a group or one-on-one setting would be best'" (footnote omitted)); *Lt. T.B. ex rel. N.B. v. Warwick School Committee*, 40 IDELR 253, 361 F.3d 80, 85 (1st Cir. 2004) (The court determined the district's IEP to be appropriate in part because its "well-trained teaching staff" had "extensive experience and training in working with autistic children"); *Michael J. v. Derry Township School Dist.*, 45

IDELR 36 (M.D. Pa. 2006) (The court determined the district's IEP to be appropriate where, among other factors, "staff and personnel undergo mandatory and optional training in educating autistic children, including training in ABA and TEACCH strategies, among others.") (Citation omitted.).)

Identify Array of Methodologies with Clear Rationale

A comprehensive program should be able to accommodate various instructional strategies and methodologies. When designing a broad-based program for children with autism spectrum disorders, districts should identify an array of instructional methodologies for use within such a program and have a clear rationale for the use of each one. This will help enable staff members to both soundly apply the methods and clearly articulate their rationale for doing so.

As noted earlier, the dispute in *J.P. ex rel. Popson v. West Clark Community Schools*, 38 IDELR 5, 230 F. Supp. 2d 910 (S.D. Ind. 2002), centered around the provision of special education services to a preschool-age child with severe autism. Following J.P.'s diagnosis of autism at age 2, as well as extensive evaluation by the district upon his enrollment for preschool at age 3, a Case Conference Committee (CCC) was convened in January 2000 with the parents to develop an IEP for him. At a subsequent meeting in April 2000, the CCC met again to review J.P.'s progress and establish new goals. At that time, "J.P.'s weakest point seemed to be his functional communication skills, encompassing expressive and receptive communication." The CCC agreed to provide ESY services to J.P. to avoid substantial regression in his communication skills, consisting of a total of weekly one-hour speech therapy sessions for eight weeks. The sufficiency of these ESY services appears to have been an early point of contention between the parents (who believed that regression occurred due to insufficiency of these services) and the district (which asserted that the services provided were adequate to prevent or minimize regression).

The dispute continued to heat up. At the August 2000 CCC meeting to determine J.P.'s IEP for the following year, the parents expressed concern about what they perceived to be their son's lack of progress and requested at least 25 hours per week of direct one-on-one instruction with "a blend of preschool programming." The district agreed to provide more direct instruction, though they increased J.P.'s special education instruction to 20 hours per week rather than the 25 or more hours requested by the parents. The district implemented this IEP using an "eclectic" instructional approach, which combined elements of different methodologies.

The methodologies used by the district soon became a focal point of contention, as the parents, after engaging the services of a private organization in fall 2000 to provide a supplementary at-home program for their son consisting of ABA/DTT methodology, began to press for exclusive use of ABA methodology with J.P. The methodology dispute intensified, ultimately resulting in the parents filing a request for a due process hearing to challenge the district's program. The hearing officer decided the case in the district's favor on many issues, and when the parents appealed the matter to federal district court, the court granted the school district's motion for summary judgment. Crucial to the court's decision was that

> West Clark school personnel were able to articulate the principles involved [in their chosen methodologies]. For example, J.P.'s speech therapist testified that, by using ABA/DTT methods, J.P. had made substantial progress in learning to vocalize. But she pointed out that he still was not communicating because he had not yet grasped the communicative intent of the sounds he was making. Her testimony made clear that she understood the difference between "vocalizing" and "communicating," and believed that the overarching goal of achieving functional communication would be best facilitated by means other than just discrete trial training. The Court cannot say whether this is a correct educational analysis, but it is certainly a rational one.

What was compelling to the court was the fact that key district personnel had and could articulate a firm understanding of the theoretical underpinnings of the methodologies in question.

The *Deal* case discussed earlier in this chapter also reflects judicial consideration and approval of school district personnel's understanding of the methodologies they used. As explained, that case eventually reached the 6th Circuit Court of Appeals, which in 2004 remanded the matter in part back to the district court to decide whether the school district had offered an IEP that was reasonably calculated to provide meaningful educational benefit to Zachary.

On remand, the district court found that the school district had offered an IEP to Zachary that was reasonably calculated to provide a meaningful educational benefit, and thus no substantive violation had occurred. This ruling was later affirmed in 2008, again by the 6th Circuit Court of Appeals. (*See Deal v. Hamilton County Dep't of Educ.*, 46 IDELR 45 (E.D. Tenn. 2006), *aff'd*, 49 IDELR 123 (6th Cir. 2008).) As the district court's analysis (on remand) makes clear, one of the factors that weighed in the school district's favor was the fact that school district witnesses were able to articulate their rationale for implementing the district's chosen methodologies:

> Ms. Chapman, the HCDE director of exceptional education, testified regarding HCDE's methodologies for [Zachary]:
>
> > The school's programs for [Zachary] offered a developmental curriculum based on two known and established sequence of objectives or curriculum. . . . [T]he most powerful part of the school's IEP to me at least without question is the fact that it had strong methodologies to train [Zachary] or to assist [Zachary] in meeting communication intent and socialization, which from my experience of thirty years, is essential for school achievement and for a quality of life that we want for everyone.

In a methodology dispute, a school district's position is strengthened when, in the context of a comprehensive program for children with autism spectrum disorders, school district personnel have a clear understanding of and rationale for the use of their chosen methodologies, and can articulate that rationale.

Every district should engage in program design and development whether or not they currently are serving identified children with autism spectrum disorders within the school system. Keeping in mind the breadth of what constitutes a FAPE for children with autism spectrum disorders, districts should be prepared to deliver a comprehensive program of services to these children. The essential components of such a program should be assured, regardless of instructional methodology, and school personnel should be well-prepared (including through ongoing training and support) to implement such a program. Within the context of the comprehensive program that conforms to state requirements and standards, school districts should identify an array of methodologies for use within their comprehensive program and have a clear rationale for their use.

The IDEA 2004, its implementing regulations, and accompanying discussion by the USDE regarding the regulations together provide a framework to guide methodology selection: it must be based on peer-reviewed research to the extent practicable. Chapter 4 prepares school districts to make methodological choices within the context of the new IDEA.

ENDNOTES

[1] National Research Council. (2001). *Educating children with autism*. 140. Committee on Educational Interventions for Children with Autism. Catherine Lord and James P. McGee, eds. Division of Behavioral and Social Sciences and Education. Washington, D.C.: National Academy Press.

[2] Myers, Scott M., M.D. (2007). Management of children with autism spectrum disorders. *Pediatrics*, vol. 120: num. 5:1163-64.

[3] Myers, Scott M., M.D. (2007). Management of children with autism spectrum disorders. *Pediatrics,* vol. 120: num. 5:1163.

[4] *Amanda J. ex rel. Annette J. v. Clark County Sch. Dist.*, 103 LRP 33278, 267 F.3d 877, 883 (9th Cir. 2001) (citation omitted).

[5] U.S. Government Accountability Office. *Special education: Children with autism*, 36. Washington, D.C., January 2005.

[6] U.S. Government Accountability Office. *Special education: Children with autism*, 30. Washington, D.C., January 2005.

[7] *Board of Educ. v. Rowley*, 553 IDELR 656 (EHLR 553:656), 458 U.S. 176, 207 (1982).

[8] *J.P. ex rel. Popson v. West Clark Community Schs.*, 38 IDELR 5, 230 F. Supp. 2d 910, 938 (S.D. Ind. 2002).

[9] *Deal v. Hamilton County Dep't of Educ.,* 46 IDELR 45 (E.D. Tenn. 2006), *aff'd*, 49 IDELR 123 (6th Cir. 2008). Various issues in this case, including the issue of predetermination, are discussed in upcoming chapters.

[10] *Id.*

[11] *Id.*

Chapter 4

Methodology Selection for Children with Autism Spectrum Disorders

What the Research Says

Despite the growing body of research to support the development and refinement of various instructional methodologies for children with autism spectrum disorders, the 2001 National Research Council report stated:

> There is a need for well-controlled clinical outcome research on these and other models of service delivery. . . . [T]he research to date is not at a level of experimental sophistication that permits unequivocal statements on the efficacy of a given approach. . . . There is no outcome study published in a peer-reviewed journal that supports comparative statements of the superiority of one model or approach over another.[1]

In 2007, the American Academy of Pediatrics reported on the results of limited early comparative studies, but cautioned that definitive outcomes remain elusive:

> Proponents of behavior analytic approaches have been the most active in using scientific methods to evaluate their work, and most studies of comprehensive treatment programs that meet minimal scientific standards involve treatment of preschoolers using behavioral approaches. However, there is still a need for additional research, including large controlled studies with randomization and assessment of treatment fidelity. Empirical scientific support for developmental models and other interventions is more limited, and well-controlled systematic studies of efficacy are needed.

> Most educational programs available to young children with ASDs are based in their communities, and often, an "eclectic" treatment approach is used, which draws on a combination of methods including applied behavior analytic methods such as DTT; structured teaching procedures; speech-language therapy, with or without picture communication or related augmentative or alternative communication strategies; SI therapy; and typical preschool activities. Three studies that compared intensive ABA programs (25-40 hours/week) to equally intensive eclectic approaches have suggested that ABA programs were significantly more effective. Another study that involved children with ASDs and global developmental delay/mental retardation retrospectively compared a less intensive ABA program (mean: 12 hours) to a comparably intensive eclectic approach and found statistically significant but clinically modest outcomes that favored those in the ABA group. Although the groups of children were similar on key dependent measures before treatment began, these studies were limited because of parent-determined rather than random assignment to treatment group. Additional studies to evaluate and compare educational treatment approaches are warranted.[2]

Why the Research Matters

"Based on Peer-Reviewed Research to the Extent Practicable"

The 2007 clinical report from the American Academy of Pediatrics opines that "[a]ll treatments [for children with autism spectrum disorders], including educational interventions, should be based on sound theoretical constructs, rigorous methodologies, and empirical studies of efficacy." The IDEA 2004 echoes this emphasis on high-quality empirical research, but its mandate does not extend quite so far.

The IDEA 2004 requires that each child's IEP contain "[a] statement of the special education and related services and supplementary aids and services, *based on peer-reviewed research to the extent practicable*, to be provided to the child. . . ." 34 CFR 300.320(a)(4) (emphasis added). What does this requirement mean, and how does it apply to instructional methodologies for children with autism spectrum disorders?

The IDEA does not define "peer-reviewed research," but the ESEA, as amended by the NCLB, defines "scientifically based research," which includes peer-reviewed research, as follows:

> The term "scientifically based research" —
>
> (A) means research that involves the application of rigorous, systematic, and objective procedures to obtain reliable and valid knowledge relevant to education activities and programs; and
>
> (B) includes research that —
>
>> (i) employs systematic, empirical methods that draw on observation or experiment;
>>
>> (ii) involves rigorous data analyses that are adequate to test the stated hypotheses and justify the general conclusions drawn;
>>
>> (iii) relies on measurements or observational methods that provide reliable and valid data across evaluators and observers, across multiple measurements and observations, and across studies by the same or different investigators;
>>
>> (iv) is evaluated using experimental or quasi-experimental designs in which individuals, entities, programs, or activities are assigned to different conditions and with appropriate controls to evaluate the effects of the condition of interest, with a preference for random-assignment experiments, or other designs to the extent that those designs contain within-condition or across-condition controls;
>>
>> (v) ensures that experimental studies are presented in sufficient detail and clarity to allow for replication or, at a minimum, offer the opportunity to build systematically on their findings; and
>>
>> (vi) has been accepted by a *peer-reviewed* journal or approved by a panel of independent experts through a comparably rigorous, objective, and scientific review.

20 USC 7801(37) (emphasis added).

The USDE declined to define "peer-reviewed research" in the federal regulations. In its discussion of the final IDEA 2004 regulations, the USDE provided limited interpretation:

> "Peer-reviewed research" generally refers to research that is reviewed by qualified and independent reviewers to ensure that the quality of the information meets the standards of the field before the research is published. However, there is no single definition of "peer-reviewed research" because the review process varies depending on the type of information to be reviewed. We believe it beyond the scope of these regulations to include a specific definition of "peer-reviewed research" and the various processes used for peer reviews.

71 Fed. Reg. 46,664 (2006).

In its discussion of the regulations, the USDE further distinguished "peer-reviewed research" from other common phrases used in the field, "evidenced-based practices" and "emerging best practices," as follows:

> The [IDEA] does not refer to "evidenced-based practices" or "emerging best practices," which are generally terms of art that may or may not be based on peer-reviewed research.

71 Fed. Reg. 46,665 (2006).

Finally the USDE, in its discussion of the regulations, described a limited circumstance when a district would be excused from providing services based on "peer-reviewed research" as follows:

> The phrase "to the extent practicable," as used in this context, generally means that services and supports should be based on peer-reviewed research to the extent that it is possible, given the availability of peer-reviewed research. We do not believe further clarification is necessary.
>
> . . .
>
> . . . States, school districts, and school personnel must, therefore, select and use methods that research has shown to be effective, to the extent that methods based on peer-reviewed research are available.
>
> . . .
>
> . . . If no such [peer-reviewed] research exists, the service may still be provided, if the IEP Team determines that such services are appropriate.

71 Fed. Reg. 46,665 (2006).

What the above discussion suggests is that the USDE believes the "availability" of peer-reviewed research makes the use of it legally practicable, and the absence of peer-reviewed research makes the use of it legally not practicable.

The IDEA requirements do not specify which instructional methodologies for children with autism spectrum disorders school districts should use. This makes sense, given the evolving nature of research on autism spectrum disorder methodologies — and given the well-established principle of *individualized* education required under the IDEA. The USDE in its discussion of the regulations emphasizes what also is clear in the case law:

37

States, school districts, and school personnel must . . . select and use methods that research has shown to be effective, to the extent that methods based on peer-reviewed research are available. This does not mean that the service with the greatest body of research is the service necessarily required for a child to receive FAPE. Likewise, there is nothing in the Act to suggest that the failure of a public agency to provide services based on peer-reviewed research would automatically result in a denial of FAPE. The final decision about the special education and related services, and supplementary aids and services that are to be provided to a child must be made by the child's IEP team based on the child's individual needs.

71 Fed. Reg. 46,665 (2006).

In cases involving autism spectrum disorder methodology disputes, courts have typically emphasized the centrality of individualized instruction insofar as they generally refuse to compare the relative merits of two different methodologies in an abstract sense. Instead, they focus on whether or not a district's challenged methodology is reasonably calculated to provide a FAPE to the student in question. (*See, e.g., Lt. T.B. ex rel. N.B. v. Warwick Sch. Committee*, 40 IDELR 253, 361 F.3d 80, 86 (1st Cir. 2004) ("Once the determination is made that the IEP was adequate, that ends the inquiry. We need not consider whether other programs would be better."); *see also Z.F. v. South Harrison Community Sch. Corp.*, 106 LRP 34735, Not Reported in F. Supp. 2d, 10 (S.D. Ind. 2005) ("A comparison of the two programs is irrelevant except to the extent it sheds light on the adequacy or inadequacy of the district's program. The inquiry is whether the district's program in substance complied with the IDEA.").)

In *Beth B. v. Van Clay*, 35 IDELR 150, 211 F. Supp. 2d 1020 (N.D. Ill. 2001), *aff'd*, 36 IDELR 121, 282 F.3d 493 (7th Cir. 2002), *cert. denied*, 537 U.S. 948 (2002), the school district was faced with the challenge of providing services to a student with Rett Syndrome, a disorder which "is characterized in the American Psychological Association *Diagnostic and Statistical Manual IV* as a form of autism, resulting in severe to profound disabilities to motor functioning, communication and cognition." One of the primary difficulties for the district was the fact that only limited information existed regarding the disorder. The court agreed with the hearing officer's conclusion that the district had properly conducted its own careful review and consideration of the available research in developing this student's IEP:

We must . . . consider that the scientific and educational communities have only a limited understanding of Rett Syndrome. Because its incidence is so low, there have not been sufficient studies to determine, to any degree of certainty, how to best educate students with this disorder.

. . . The studies completed thus far have been limited in scope and the theories they developed have not been sufficiently tested to reach any authoritative conclusions. Given these limits, the district consulted with some of the most knowledgeable experts available. Plaintiffs make much of the fact that the district agreed to consult an independent expert, Dr. Joseph Vaal, in developing Beth's IEP, but then did not follow his recommendations. The district, in fact, consulted with multiple "experts." Besides Dr. Vaal, the district also consulted with Dr. Richard Van Acker, who reached very different conclusions. The district's special education teachers, who have experience with cognitive disabilities in general, and Beth's teachers, aides and inclusion coordinators, who have direct experience with Beth, also participated in the process. A district is not obliged to follow any particular one's advice. School officials do not relinquish their ultimate authority to make educational policy decisions by agreeing to consider an independent consultant's opinion.

What emerges from the USDE discussion and the case law is that when selecting methodologies to be utilized within the context of a comprehensive program for children with autism spectrum disorders, a school district must conduct a thorough review of the peer-reviewed research and be prepared to defend its chosen methodologies. Although the language says "to the extent practicable," we think districts are responsible for knowing what methodologies are being used, and whether the methodologies have support in the research.

When designing an *individualized* program for a specific child, however, individual factors must be taken into account that could require the use of methodologies that are not supported by peer-reviewed research. Still, the emphasis on individually tailored instruction should not be interpreted to mean that districts have unfettered latitude in making methodology choices. Given that a body of research on instructional methodologies for children with autism spectrum disorders does exist, and the peer-reviewed research is emerging, it is incumbent upon districts to use that research as a guide in making methodology selections.

Differences in Outcomes Between Methods

Thus far, those studies conducted to gauge the comparative effectiveness of different instructional methodologies have been limited in scope. However, because this research is ongoing, districts are advised to stay informed and up-to-date regarding results in this area. Although courts have historically declined to compare methodologies in the abstract in these types of disputes, they have done so primarily because their well-established role is to determine whether a district's challenged methodology is reasonably calculated to provide a FAPE to a particular child. As suggested by the 6th Circuit Court of Appeals in *Deal ex rel. Deal v. Hamilton County Board of Education*, 42 IDELR 109, 392 F.3d 840 (6th Cir. 2004), *cert. denied*, 546 U.S. 936 (2005), there may come a point when credible research indicates such a disparity in outcomes between two methodologies that a district's proposed use of a lesser methodology could constitute a denial of FAPE:

> The facile answer to the question raised by this disagreement [over the level of education that must be provided to a child with a disability under the IDEA] is that a school district is only required to provide educational programming that is reasonably calculated to enable the child to derive more than *de minimis* educational benefit. This Court and others faced with essentially the same question have decided that school systems are not required to provide autistic children with the sort of intensive (and expensive) educational program pioneered by Dr. Lovaas.

> At some point, however, this facile answer becomes insufficient. Indeed, *there is a point at which the difference in outcomes between two methods can be so great that provision of the lesser program could amount to a denial of FAPE.* (Emphasis added.)

Just a few years after having made this statement, the 6th Circuit did engage in a comparison analysis to a certain extent when it revisited the *Deal* case on appeal from the district court remand. (*See Deal ex rel. Deal v. Hamilton County Dep't of Educ.*, 49 IDELR 123 (6th Cir. 2008) ("Based on the district court's findings, we cannot say the [parents'] home program was so superior to the School System's program that refusal to fund the home program constituted a denial of a FAPE.").) However, despite the 6th Circuit's treatment of the two methodologies in that dispute, we do not believe we have yet reached the point at which research on differences between methodology outcomes is so unequivocal and compelling that courts are likely to conclude that "provision of the lesser program . . . amount[s] to a denial of FAPE." Neither the research nor the case law indicates that we have arrived at that point. Nevertheless, for all of the reasons discussed in this chapter, it is critical that districts review the available peer-reviewed research and continue to monitor the developments in this area.

Replicable Research

In the preamble to the IDEA, Congress makes the following finding:

> [T]he implementation of this title has been impeded by low expectations, and an insufficient focus on applying replicable research on proven methods of teaching and learning for children with disabilities.

20 USC 1400(c)(4).

One of the key challenges school districts face is assessing whether the research is replicable. Results yielded in a highly controlled laboratory environment are not always replicable in the natural environment. There are many variables that cannot be controlled in a public school setting, or at least not to the same degree as in a laboratory school of a university, or in some cases, in a private school setting.

The case of *L.B. and J.B. ex rel. K.B. v. Nebo School District*, 41 IDELR 206, 379 F.3d 966 (10th Cir. 2004), is an example that illustrates the way certain variables can be controlled in a private but not a public school setting. In that case, the school district did not provide preschool programs for children without disabilities. In order to provide inclusion opportunities for their preschool-age children without disabilities, the district created "mixed environments that focus[ed] on special education while incorporating some typical children." Initially, the district's program was "populated mainly by disabled students, but include[ed] thirty to fifty percent typically developing children ('typical children') who [were] present for the full length of the preschool classes." When this did not satisfy the parent's request for a mainstreamed preschool class for K.B., a preschool-age child with autism, the district offered to increase the ratio to 50 percent, but the parents declined. The experts who testified for the parents lamented that the school district's "hybrid" program of students with and without disabilities had a number of flaws, including (in pertinent part) that

> Park View's student body was predominantly male. Typically, preschool boys' social interactions are less sophisticated than those of similarly aged girls. Experts testified that K.B. would make better progress in a more gender-balanced environment, such as her mainstream private preschool, where she was exposed to the more developmentally complex social interactions in which girls engage.

This case evolved into a dispute about whether the public school, Park View, or the private preschool provided the least restrictive environment for K.B.:

> A preponderance of the evidence shows that the mainstream [private preschool] classroom provided K.B. with appropriate role models, had a more balanced gender ratio, and was generally better suited to meet K.B.'s behavioral and social needs than was Park View's hybrid classroom. [ ] Thus, this factor strongly weighs in favor of a conclusion that Park View was not K.B.'s least restrictive environment.

The 10th Circuit Court of Appeals ultimately concluded that the private preschool was the least restrictive environment. The District, therefore, was required to reimburse the parents for the ABA services they sought for K.B., and had unilaterally obtained for her, to enable her to benefit in the private preschool environment. Those services included:

> (1) forty hours per week of ABA services; (2) seven and one-half hours per week of preparation time for ABA therapists to plan for individual sessions; (3) two and one-half hours per week for a team meeting with K.B.'s five ABA therapists; (4) one day per month for an ABA consultant to train the five therapists; (5) materials

for ABA program; (6) one hour of speech therapy per week; and (7) occupational therapy as needed.

The make-up of a classroom, including the gender balance among its students, the nature and level of severity of the disabilities of the children, and the array of their various needs, are variables over which public schools have only limited control. Thus, when reviewing a methodology for possible implementation, school districts should carefully examine the number and types of variables that would need to be controlled in order to achieve the results the methodology purports to achieve. Impressive laboratory results are of little value if they cannot be replicated in the environment of a public school.

When examining the results of the research, school districts should look at whether the results were obtained in a public school setting (especially one with similar demographics). If the results were not initially obtained in a public school setting, then school districts should investigate whether these results have subsequently been replicated in a public school setting. If there are no studies that have yielded comparable results in a public school setting, then the school district needs to carefully examine whether that method is or might be readily replicable.

Eclectic Approaches

As illustrated in the *Popson* and *Deal* cases, one of the programming issues a district may confront is whether it is permissible to implement an eclectic approach — that is, one that combines elements of different instructional methodologies rather than using just one method exclusively. The answer from the case law so far is — it depends on how you do it. A school district's use of an eclectic approach has been regarded favorably by courts in cases in which the record showed that staff members had implemented it thoughtfully, deliberately, and with a high degree of understanding and skill.

For example, in the case of *J.P. ex rel. Popson v. West Clark Community Schs.*, 38 IDELR 5, 230 F. Supp. 2d 910 (S.D. Ind. 2002), when the district agreed to increase the amount of J.P.'s direct instruction to 20 hours per week under a revised IEP, it

> implemented the revised IEP using what it acknowledged to be an "eclectic" approach that incorporated PECS, one-on-one instruction, and some ABA/DTT techniques, together with an attempt to include J.P. with the other kids in the preschool program.

> The instructional approach used by J.P.'s teachers has been described as "eclectic." Instructional staff and specialists use a variety of techniques that are deemed developmentally appropriate for the child. Many of these techniques have been advocated by TEACCH, a nationally known program for children with autism.

The appropriateness of this approach was challenged by the parents, who in the fall of 2000 engaged a private organization (BIFAC) to provide a supplementary at-home program of ABA/DTT methodology for J.P. They came to believe that their son was making better progress with the BIFAC program than he was with the district's program. As a result, they asked the district "to fund at least 40 hours per week of combined home and school training, under the supervision of BIFAC personnel, with an emphasis upon verbal behavior." The district rejected that request, concluding:

> 20 hours would suffice, based upon J.P.'s past progress. Similarly, West Clark rejected the Popsons' request for an IEP based exclusively upon ABA/DTT methods, finding that J.P. had made significant progress during the school year under West Clark's more eclectic approach.

The district court found *West Clark*'s eclectic approach to be appropriate. Its explanation of its reasoning includes a helpful contrast between the facts of this case and the facts in *T.H. and L.H. and*

S.H. v. Board of Education of Palatine Community Consolidated School District 15, 103 LRP 38770, 55 F. Supp. 2d 830 (N.D. Ill. 1999), in which the school district's "eclectic" approach was found to be inadequate:

> . . . The *Palatine* court found that, despite their discomfort with the ABA/DTT approach, school district staff could not "articulate a particular methodology which they prefer[red]." . . . [T]he court further noted that [the student's] classroom teacher uses an educational method she calls "floor times," which she described as "following the child's lead;" however, she could "not explain how this generic approach could be effective for autistic children . . . who have problems 'attending.'"

> . . . The *Palatine* court further noted that the IEP itself could "best be described as a work in progress." While the case conference committee set "a number of appropriate goals" for [the student], the court found that school district personnel did not have a clear idea how to achieve those goals or measure progress toward those goals and believed that that was something to be worked out "after personnel in the early childhood program 'take a good look on a day-to-day basis.'"

> . . .

> The facts in [this] case are quite different. First, even if the approaches of the two school districts are both properly characterized as eclectic, that does not make them the same. Unlike the Palatine school district, West Clark incorporated a number of hours of one-on-one time into its curriculum for J.P. During that time . . . they did use ABA/DTT methods. The fact that school officials also believed that a certain amount of group time was appropriate for J.P., because learning occurs in context, does not mean that they relied solely, or even primarily, upon unstructured group time. Moreover, West Clark did not just throw J.P. into a normal pre-school group, as appears to have been the case with [the student in *Palatine*].

> . . . Unlike the Palatine school district, West Clark proposed to use a variety of techniques that were specifically designed for autistic children. As J.P.'s classroom teacher testified, these techniques included PECS and one-on-one ABA/DTT training, as well as group time designed to bring J.P. into the general preschool program. This is a far more articulated approach than the notion offered by [the student's] teacher [in *Palatine*] of "floor times" that are "child led."

The deliberate care and skill that West Clark demonstrated in developing J.P.'s program in the *Popson* case, including the "eclectic" methodologies to be used within the context of its comprehensive program, stands in clear contrast to the other district's ill-defined "eclectic" approach in the *Palatine* case. This difference was essential to the *Popson* court's determination that this eclectic approach was appropriate for J.P.

A similar point was made in the *Deal, supra*, district court case on remand.[3] That case also involved a methodology dispute in which the school district proposed a comprehensive program, which included the use of eclectic methodologies while the parents objected, seeking to have an exclusive ABA methodology implemented instead. The Memorandum Opinion issued by the district court in the *Deal* remand includes extensive discussion of the district's eclectic methodologies. That court ultimately determined that the school district's comprehensive program, including its selection of methodologies, was reasonably calculated to provide Zachary with a FAPE, based on several factors.

First, the school district's approach combined elements from several identifiable, research-based, well-regarded methodologies for children with autism spectrum disorders. As testified to by district personnel, the district combined these elements in a deliberate manner tailored to Zachary's unique needs, and did not just use a "grab bag" of randomly chosen programmatic elements:

> The program [for Zachary] used a variety of integrated methodologies. . . . It's a deliberate integrated set of methodologies for a given student that might be effective and it included speech therapy both within the classroom setting and outside the classroom setting. . . .

> . . . [I]n the preschool CDC class, "we were choosing the best of a multitude of many different approaches."

> . . . PATHS . . . incorporates some elements of TEACCH, a recognized methodology for teaching autistic students, but PATHS "expanded the play and leisure segments of TEACCH and how to generalize that into the community and how to make it functional in the community." HCDE also provided evidence that it used such methodologies as "discrete trial methodologies, structured teaching, incidental learning, activity-based instruction, and total communication approach."

> [The district] presented evidence of its blend of appropriate methodologies that were tailored to the needs of each individual child and evidence of the qualifications of its educators. It presented evidence of identifiable methodologies that it uses in its programs, including PATHS, DTT, PECS, structured teaching, and incidental teaching.

(*See also Michael J. v. Derry Twp. Sch. Dist.*, 45 IDELR 36 (M.D. Pa. 2006) (The court concluded that the eclectic "strategies the district contemplated using with [the student] were meaningful, sufficiently intense, and reasonably designed to assist [him to] succeed in an educational environment," noting staff testimony that they would not "just be 'picking and choosing' random strategies to implement specific goals and objectives . . . [I]t is . . . our duty to remain abreast of all new methodologies in the area of autism, and it's not just picking and choosing as though we have no-willy-nilly. It is matching the presentation or the testing to whatever the child needs to attain their goal.").)

Second, the district court in the *Deal* remand determined that a comprehensive program, which included eclectic methodologies, if implemented appropriately, was consistent with the fundamental IDEA principle that each child's educational program must be tailored to meet his or her unique needs. The Memorandum Opinion cites to certain earlier cases in support of this position:

> With respect to methodologies, Dr. Freeman testified that "the eclectic approach is the only way that truly provides individualization, whatever eclectic means because that way you're not driven by an approach and does the child learn by this approach, but you've got an armamentarium of knowledge."

> Plaintiffs in *Z.F. v. South Harrison Comm. Sch. Corp.*, 106 LRP 34735 (S.D. Ind. 2005), argued that the school district's autism program proposed for the student was "impermissibly eclectic." However, the court responded that "this kind of flexible and varied approach is consistent with the IDEA's requirement that education-

al approaches be tailored to a child's individual needs. The IDEA does not specify any particular methodology and does not prohibit the use of multiple methods," the ruling said. *See also J.K. v. Metropolitan Sch. Dist. Southwest Allen Cty.*, 44 IDELR 122 (N.D. Ind. 2005) (affirming determination that autistic student was not denied FAPE by district's refusal to supply student with 40 hours of ABA in-home methodology); *Adams v. State of Oregon*, 31 IDELR 130, 195 F.3d 1141, 1149 (9th Cir. 1999) (noting that although Lovaas program is an excellent program, "there are many available programs which effectively help develop autistic children" and relying on Dawson & Osterling article also relied upon by HCDE in this case); *Dong v. Board of Educ. of the Rochester Comm. Schs.*, 31 IDELR 157, 197 F.3d 793, 803 (6th Cir. 1999) (finding that crux of dispute over IEP resulted from debate over competing methodologies of TEACCH program and DTT program, but district's failure to implement parents' requested DTT program did not fail to take into account student's unique needs).

The 6th Circuit Court of Appeals, in affirming this ruling in 2008, upheld the appropriateness of the school district's approach for Zachary, stating that "different methodologies may be appropriate for treating autism and provide a FAPE as long as the student's individual needs are considered and the program is reasonably calculated to provide educational benefit."[4]

Within the context of a comprehensive program for a child with an autism spectrum disorder, case law supports the thoughtful use of eclectic approaches when carefully crafted and skillfully implemented. However, as the research evolves, new information may reshape the extent to which methodologies can be combined. Fidelity issues should be considered when using an eclectic approach. Moreover, it is recommended that a systematic approach to documenting progress be in place in order to ensure the appropriateness of eclectic approaches.

Predetermination

At the program design and development stage, school districts also are cautioned to avoid the pitfall of predetermination — i.e., making decisions as to which methodology or methodologies to offer children within its comprehensive program, without the flexibility to consider each child's individual needs.

Given the financial cost involved in implementing some of the best-known instructional methodologies for children with autism spectrum disorders, it is understandable that school districts might be inclined to channel their resources into a single methodology or to avoid providing certain methodologies at all. However, although case law recognizes that districts may take cost into account in determining special education services, districts may not prioritize financial considerations over their obligations under the IDEA. (*See, e.g., Renner v. Board of Educ. of Public Schs. of City of Ann Arbor*, 103 LRP 43313, 185 F.3d 635, 644 (6th Cir. 1999) ("[T]he potential financial burdens imposed on participating States may be relevant to arriving at a sensible construction of the IDEA. . . ." (citation omitted).)

Again, the *Deal* 2004 Circuit Court case helps illustrate this point. The 6th Circuit Court of Appeals, before remanding the case to the district court to determine whether Zachary's IEP was substantively appropriate, ruled in favor of the parents on the issue of whether the district had improperly predetermined the instructional methodology for implementing Zachary's IEP. Although the record demonstrated that the parents had been given the opportunity to express their opinion and present evidence at IEP team meetings concerning their request for implementation of an exclusive ABA methodology, the court found that this was essentially pretense on the district's part. The court concluded that the district's true intent all along was to offer one and only one instructional methodology — its own — regardless of Zachary's unique needs. In the court's terms, the district had an "unofficial policy" of refusing to provide one-on-one ABA methodology because it previously had invested in another methodology. This was held to constitute predetermination, which violated the IDEA by denying the child the individually tailored services to which he was entitled and by preventing the parents from having a meaningful opportunity to participate in the development of their child's IEP:

> The evidence reveals that the School System, and its representatives, had pre-decided not to offer Zachary intensive ABA services regardless of any evidence concerning Zachary's individual needs and the effectiveness of his private program. This predetermination amounted to a procedural violation of the IDEA. Because it effectively deprived Zachary's parents of meaningful participation in the IEP process, the predetermination caused substantive harm and therefore deprived Zachary of a FAPE.

> . . .

> The facts of this case strongly suggest that the School System had an unofficial policy of refusing to provide one-on-one ABA programs and that School System personnel thus did not have open minds and were not willing to consider the provision of such a program. . . . Several comments made by School System personnel suggested that they would like to provide Zachary with ABA services, i.e., they recognized the efficacy of such a program, but they were prevented from doing so, i.e., by the School System policy.

> . . . Despite the protestations of the Deals, the School System never even treated a one-on-one ABA program as a viable option. Where there was no way that anything the Deals said, or any data the Deals produced, could have changed the School System's determination of appropriate services, their participation was no more than after the fact involvement.

> . . .

> The School System seemed to suggest, at oral argument, that it is entitled to invest in a program such as TEACCH and then capitalize on that investment by using the TEACCH program exclusively. But this is precisely what it is not permitted to do, at least without fully considering the individual needs of each child. A school district unquestionably may consider cost in determining appropriate services for a child. The school district is required, however, to base its placement decision on the child's IEP . . . rather than on the mere fact of a pre-existing investment. In other words, the school district may not, as it appears happened here, decide that because it has spent a lot of money on a program, that program is always going to be appropriate for educating children with a specific disability, *regardless of any evidence to the contrary of the individualized needs of a particular child.* A placement decision may only be considered to have been based on the child's IEP when the child's individual characteristics, including demonstrated response to particular types of educational programs, are taken into account. A "one size fits all" approach to special education will not be countenanced by the IDEA.[5] (Emphasis in the original.)

The way to avoid improper predetermination is to design and develop a comprehensive program without regard to methodology. The program should contain the essential components of a program for children with autism spectrum disorders, as established by the research. Such a program provides the structure within which a variety of sound methodologies can be implemented. Within this framework, the school district should:

- consider an array of methodologies to be utilized within the context of a comprehensive program;

- know the research regarding the chosen methodologies;

- conduct appropriate levels of professional development so that staff is qualified to select, tailor and implement an array of methodologies; and

- implement methodologies based on peer-reviewed research to the extent practicable.

Chapter 5 provides a case-based introduction to certain methodologies that have been the subject of many recent legal disputes, both to familiarize readers with key aspects of those methods and to illustrate what it is about particular methodologies that has generated controversy.

ENDNOTES

[1] National Research Council. (2001). *Educating children with autism.* 166. Committee on Educational Interventions for Children with Autism. Catherine Lord and James P. McGee, eds. Division of Behavioral and Social Sciences and Education. Washington, D.C.: National Academy Press.

[2] Myers, Scott M., M.D. (2007). Management of children with autism spectrum disorders. *Pediatrics*, vol. 120: num. 5:1166.

[3] *Deal v. Hamilton County Dep't of Educ.*, 46 IDELR 45 (E.D. Tenn. 2006), *aff'd*, 108 LRP 1858 (6th Cir. 2008).

[4] *Deal ex rel. Deal v. Hamilton County Dep't of Educ.*, 49 IDELR 123 (6th Cir. 2008).

[5] *Deal ex. rel. v. Hamilton County Bd. of Educ.*, 42 IDELR 109, 392 F.3d 840, 857-59 (6th Cir. 2004), *cert. denied*, 546 U.S. 936 (2005). Note that this finding of a procedural violation was not fatal to the district's IEP for Zachary or for its ultimate ability to implement its chosen methodology, as the district's IEP was ultimately affirmed as appropriate by the district court on remand and the 6th Circuit in 2008.

Chapter 5

What to Keep in Mind When Reading the Cases

This book is based on the premise that court cases are valuable sources of information regarding what to do and what not to do, from a legal perspective, with respect to educating children with autism spectrum disorders. Naturally, many of the cases we discuss and quote include descriptions of some of the features of instructional methodologies that have been the subject of litigation. However, although these cases shed light on what constitutes a sound program from a legal perspective and what makes a school district's chosen methodology legally defensible at the selection phase and the implementation phase, readers should not treat the methodology descriptions in published cases as a substitute for a careful review of the research regarding methodologies for children with autism spectrum disorders.

Key Points for Reading Cases

Case-Based Descriptions of Methodology Features Give Only a Partial Picture

Disputes under the IDEA begin at the administrative due process hearing level, and most or all of the evidence in such cases is typically presented at this level. When these disputes are appealed to federal district and appellate courts, those courts generally rely on the record established at the administrative level, admitting new evidence only as needed. The reviewing courts therefore are largely limited by the extent of the existing administrative record, including the extent to which it includes descriptions of and explanations regarding the disputed methodologies. Furthermore, reviewing courts then sift through that administrative record and incorporate information into their written decisions as necessary to explain and support their analysis. Thus, readers should never assume that descriptions of methodologies in court cases are complete enough to facilitate a thorough understanding of a given methodology.

This is true even when a published court case includes expert witness testimony about the features of a particular methodology. Whether that testimony comes from the administrative record or is taken by the court itself as additional evidence, reviewing courts will only incorporate testimony into their written decisions to the extent that doing so supports their discussions of the issue(s) before them. Thus, even highly technical, detailed descriptions of methodologies are likely to provide only a partial picture.

The Role of the Courts Is Not to Compare the Efficacy of Competing Methodologies

Frequently, expert witnesses called by opposing parties in a methodology dispute will offer conflicting testimony. For example, in many of the cases discussed in this book, parents have called expert witnesses who testify that ABA is the methodology that should be used exclusively to educate a child with autism spectrum disorders. Witnesses for the district might testify that, for example, multiple methodologies combined with ABA constitute a program that offers the child a FAPE. In most cases, courts adhere to the general rule that their role is not to determine which approach is better in an abstract sense. Instead, courts focus on whether the district's program including its chosen methodologies is "reasonably calculated" to provide a FAPE to the child in question. A court will typically only assess a methodology requested by a parent if that court decides that the district's chosen methodologies do not provide a FAPE — and even then, the court will only describe the methodologies at issue to the extent necessary to support its decision in a particular case. Therefore, court decisions that present information about competing methodologies should not be considered to present a thorough and complete comparison of their strengths, weaknesses, and relative efficacy.

Court Cases Do Not Necessarily Describe the Most Current Methodologies

As explained above, disputes over methodologies for children with autism spectrum disorders begin in administrative due process hearings. It can take months or years for cases to reach the court system on appeal and to appear thereafter in court decisions. Because this book incorporates examples from court cases rather than administrative hearings (because of the relative weight of legal authority ascribed to the former), the methods discussed in these cases do not necessarily give an accurate picture of where the research has taken us in recent years in terms of available methodologies. This does not diminish the value of these cases for illustrating what factors courts consider and how courts analyze these disputes. But readers cannot rely on these descriptions to fully capture the range of, and details about, the most up-to-date methods available in this evolving field.

Case Descriptions of Certain Autism Spectrum Disorder Methodologies

Notwithstanding all of the foregoing, we think it may be useful for readers who are unfamiliar with some of the leading methodologies that have been the subject of litigation to read examples of how these methodologies have been described by the courts. The quotes below are intended to acquaint readers with the aspects of these methodologies that frequently have been the subject of legal disputes, in particular, to give readers a taste of what it is about those methodologies that has made them the subject of so much controversy. The descriptions of methodologies found in court cases also shed light on the significant level of resources required to implement many of these methodologies with fidelity.

Some methodologies are designed to combine multiple instructional strategies to address the majority of the educational needs of a child. Examples are Applied Behavioral Analysis (ABA), the Lovaas Model of Applied Behavioral Analysis, and TEACCH (Treatment and Education of Autistic and related Communication-Handicapped Children). All of these methodologies have been the subject of litigation. Other methodologies are designed to target specific areas of need, such as augmentative and alternative communication methodologies. The Picture Exchange Communication System (PECS) is one such communication methodology that has been the subject of litigation. The following descriptions are taken directly from court cases.

Applied Behavioral Analysis (ABA)

ABA is a systematic, analytical approach to addressing learning as a function of behavior that targets concrete and measurable goals, utilizes constant and consistent data to analyze what techniques are working and how, and draws upon a system of planned reinforcements to . . . [assist a child with autism to] communicate and function independently. (*Michael J. v. Derry Township Sch. Dist.*, 45 IDELR 36, Not Reported in F. Supp. 2d, 2 (M.D. Pa. 2006).)

[ABA] involves intensive one-to-one interaction between the child and a trained ABA instructor. ABA focuses on separating complex skills into their simplest discrete components, and teaching these components to the child through repetition and positive reinforcement. When the child demonstrates mastery of the components, the goal becomes to "reassemble" the components back into the more complex skill. (*Z.F. v. South Harrison Community Sch. Corp.*, 106 LRP 34735, Not Reported in F. Supp. 2d, 1 n.2 (S.D. Ind. 2005).)

During initial phases of ABA, educators and therapists rely upon Discrete Trial Training (DTT), which provides a systematic and rapid reward based training for each step of the skills being taught. ABA utilizes DTT in order to assure that a student begins to master and generalize skills in less restrictive and more natural settings. (*Michael J. v. Derry Township Sch. Dist.*, 45 IDELR 36, Not Reported in F. Supp. 2d, 2 (M.D. Pa. 2006).)

Each [discrete] trial consists of giving the child a discreet [*sic*] instruction (such as "stand up," "look at me," "touch nose," "what is your name," "what is this," "what is the boy doing," "say Daddy," identifying colors, shapes, big vs. small, etc.), waiting for a response, and then providing an appropriate . . . consequence. A single trial can last as little as 30 seconds if the child responds properly, but much longer if the trainer has to wait for the correct response. (*Renner v. Board of Educ. of Public Schs. of City of Ann Arbor*, 103 LRP 43313, 185 F.3d 635, 638 n.4 (6th Cir. 1999) (citation omitted).)

The teacher gives an instruction to the student, who responds either compliantly, non-compliantly, or with delay, and the teacher either responds immediately to correct the non-compliant response, praises and rewards an immediate compliant response, or delays the response in the case of the student's delay. Repetitive practice aims to teach the student the skill. Instructors maintain detailed data, recording each response by the student as it is made. Once several discrete skills are mastered separately, the tasks are intermingled to develop so-called "discrimination" skills. ABA is time intensive . . . [Daily teaching sessions of] six hours of ABA therapy year round would be required for [some] student[s] . . . to reach normal grade level. (*County Sch. Bd. of Henrico County, VA v. R.T.*, 45 IDELR 274, 433 F. Supp. 2d 657, 669-670 (E.D. Va. 2006).)

In order to achieve the goal of generalization, an ABA program requires implementation by a trained staff, supervision by experienced ABA consultants, and delivery in a variety of settings. (*Michael J. v. Derry Twp. Sch. Dist.*, 45 IDELR 36, Not Reported in F. Supp. 2d, 2 (M.D. Pa. 2006).)

Lovaas Model of Applied Behavioral Analysis

The Lovaas methodology was developed by Dr. Ivar Lovaas as a result of a three-year study conducted of 19 children who were diagnosed as autistic. All of the children were aged three or under and received 40 hours per week of [home-based] one-on-one instruction. . . . At the end of the study, nine of the children had achieved normal IQ's and were described as indistinguishable from their peers. Eight were placed in aphasic (communication handicapped) classes and the remaining two were in autism or special education classes.

. . . Lovaas therapy is one version of Applied Behavioral Analysis (ABA) which "consists of breaking down activities into discrete individual tasks and rewarding the child's accomplishment. The child eventually learns to integrate the information and associate instruction with a given activity." Discrete trial teaching is one aspect of the [Lovaas] program and involves a prompt to the child followed rapidly with a consequence based on whether the child gives the appropriate response. In the Lovaas program, when a child has negative behavior, the therapist analyzes why and in what context it is happening. This allows the therapist to determine the reason behind the behavior, such as seeking attention, and to predict when it will occur. Then, the therapist devises an intervention plan, a plan to stop the behavior. So, for example, if the behavior is occurring because the child is frustrated by a task, it may be that the task is too difficult and therefore, needs to be broken down.

The Lovaas program designs a treatment package for the child which begins with 40 hours per week of one-on-one instruction in the child's home. Later, more and more of the time is spent in a socialization setting of school, peer play and community activities. An essential component of the program is the involvement of the parents in the therapy so that any gains made by the child with her therapist are not lost. The parent is expected to help the child generalize the skills learned during therapy to the everyday world.

. . . The program also uses a therapy log which provides continuity among the therapists and aides involved. It is used to record behavior, skills and problem areas. It becomes a record of what a child knows and does not know. The program has [a] hierarchy of goals in different categories which are to be mastered. Once a skill is mastered, the child is moved on to a new one. If he or she regresses, the therapist goes back to the last skill. The ultimate goal is for the child to generalize the skills learned in therapy. Thus, drills are used to teach the children. The Lovaas program relies on prompts to ensure that the child acquires a skill and remains successful with it. "But the goal is to start with the prompt and then fade out the prompt and get rid of it so the child is working independently." Successes are reinforced, usually by physical contact or food. Eighty percent of the Lovaas program focuses on the development of language skills. Typically, the program begins around age three and continues until seven or eight. (*CM by JM and EM v. Board of Pub. Educ. of Henderson County*, 36 IDELR 96, 184 F. Supp. 2d 466, 473-74 (W.D.N.C. 2002) (internal citations omitted).)

TEACCH (Treatment and Education of Autistic and Related Communication-Handicapped Children)

The premise of TEACCH is to utilize the typical strengths of children with autism, including visual learning, visual cues and visual scheduling, to develop other related skills that are generally more challenging. The program emphasizes a variety of communication skills and socialization, all aimed at helping the child "generalize" skills that are fostered in her educational environment. TEACCH also employs behavioral intervention, incidental teaching through various structured activities, and the Picture Exchange Communication System. Because autistic children typically have difficulty with change and uncertainty, a TEACCH program is designed with predictability in mind. (*Pitchford ex rel. M. v. Salem-Keizer Sch. Dist. No. 24J*, 35 IDELR 126, 155 F. Supp. 2d 1213, 1217 (D.C. Ore. 2001) (citation and footnote omitted).)

The TEACCH program creates a classroom environment for [children with autism] which is predictable and therefore understandable. Structure is very important to [children with autism] because they cannot handle numerous stimuli at once. The physical space of [the] classroom is arranged in a manner that explains to the child what will happen in different parts of the learning program. Thus, the child [with autism], who has strong visual skills, is able to rely on those skills to feel comfortable with the setting. The program also relies on structure in the form of a daily schedule because [children with autism] have difficulty understanding the concept of time. The daily schedule is presented to the child according to each child's abilities. Thus, some may be written and others may rely on color cues. But the purpose of the schedule is to allow the child to know in detail what will occur at each portion of the day. This is done because [children with autism] do not understand the concept of sequencing and become very anxious about what will occur next in their day. Each child has an individual work system which is designed to help the child become independent in carrying out his assignments. Within this work system are four questions for each child to integrate during his assignment: What am I supposed to do?; How long will the work last?; How do I know when I am finished?; and What comes next? The program uses visual cues as well as teacher directives. This increases independence and reduces frustration caused by an inability to understand auditory directives. Like Lovaas therapy, TEACCH allows the child to learn one task which has been broken into its simplest parts before going on to a more difficult task.

Another aspect of the program involves teaching language and communication skills. . . . This requires having the child learn and understand that communication involves two or more people. . . . The first goal is to get communication going in any form as long as there is a connection between the child and the teacher or peers. This requires an assessment of the child's current skills in order to know how to elicit spontaneous communication. Usually this is done by involving the child in an activity which interests him, such as a picture exchange in which the child names the object.

The TEACCH method does not use behavior modification to deal with behavior problems because that method is a consequential approach. Instead, it uses behavior management which means that, based on the child's individual needs, the environment is structured to prevent problems. Despite these measures, if the child exhibits aggressive or self-injurious behavior, a new assessment is done. It may be that too much is being expected of the child or it may be necessary to use a consequential approach in close proximity to the behavior. Many behavior problems in [children with autism], as with normal children, are alternative forms of communication. They are signs of stress or frustration. So, for example, rather than placing a child in a "time out" each time he kicks, he will be rewarded each time he does not kick. But the root of the solution is a determination of why the behavior occurs. Only in this manner can you eliminate the need for the behavior rather than simply suppressing the behavior itself. A child may behave with tantrums if he or she is frustrated at a task, the task has been going on too long, or it is too difficult. Although some people call it a form of task avoidance, one must understand why the child wants to avoid the task in order to understand the cause of the behavior.

. . . TEACCH views each [child with autism] as having individual differences. "[W]hile you can improve on them and help and move people along in some cases to the point that they might be indistinguishable from normal, [TEACCH] doesn't really [ ] accept the notion that everything is fixable and that autism is merely a collection of unusual behavior or behaviors and deficits." Moreover, TEACCH provides a predictable environment to enable the child to become independent by learning. . . . TEACCH uses developmental psychology to ensure that the child "crawls before he walks" rather than teaching the child to walk when he does not understand the concept of crawling. (*CM by JM and EM v. Board of Pub. Educ. of Henderson County*, 36 IDELR 96, 184 F. Supp. 2d 466, 474-76 (W.D.N.C. 2002) (internal citations omitted).)

Picture Exchange Communication System (PECS)

PECS is a system of communication marketed by Pyramid Services, Inc., which can be used as an alternative to verbal speech. It involves the use of a book filled with removable icons (pictures) printed on separate cards. In a series of steps, a child is taught first to request an item by presenting the appropriate icon, and, later, to make more sophisticated statements.

More specifically, PECS is taught in six phases. . . . At the first phase, a student is taught to deliver a single picture to a listener in order to request a specific item. One adult is needed to act as the listener, and a second adult is needed to prompt the student to select and deliver the picture. When this is mastered, it is attempted at Phase Two to teach the student to travel independently to get a picture and to approach a listener who is not directly in front of the student. At first, the prompter assists the student with this.

Phase Two is described as an ongoing phase, because once skills taught in later phases are mastered, the student will then need to be taught to travel independently to instigate those more advanced skills. Clearly, it is the recognition of PECS as a mode of communication, as acquired in Phase Two, which makes PECS a true communication system.

In the first part of Phase Three, the student learns to choose the correct picture rather than a "distractor picture" of a non-desired item. In the second part of Phase Three, the student chooses between two pictures of desired items. At Phase Four, the student is taught to construct sentences with PECS icons, using not only pictures of items, but symbols for "sentence starters" such as "I want." (*Andrew M. and Dierdre M. v. Delaware County Office of Mental Health and Mental Retardation*, 44 IDELR 92, Not Reported in F. Supp. 2d, 3 (E.D. Pa. 2005) (internal citations omitted).)

Phases Four through Six deal with more advanced sentence structure, where the child places the picture card within a sentence strip to form complete phrases, uses sentence strips to respond to questions, and finally, uses the picture cards to make general comments not in response to questions. (*R.L. by Mr. and Mrs. L. v. Plainville Bd. of Educ.*, 43 IDELR 57, 363 F. Supp. 2d 222, 232 (D.C. Conn. 2005) (citation omitted).)

Allocating Adequate Resources

As previously stated, a review of court cases, including descriptions of instructional methodologies found in court cases, should not be considered an adequate substitute for a review of the professional literature. In particular, it should not substitute for a review of the peer-reviewed research that can help school districts design and develop a comprehensive program for children with autism spectrum disorders including identifying an array of sound methodologies that may be implemented within the context of the comprehensive program. Court cases do, however, help school districts identify and understand what constitutes a sound program from a legal perspective and what makes a school district's chosen methodology legally defensible at the selection phase and the implementation phase.

The case-based descriptions of methodologies also illustrate that successful programming including implementation of methodologies for children with autism spectrum disorders requires a significant allocation of resources. Through a review of the research, school districts should carefully examine the features of the methodologies so that when a methodology is selected for a given child, the proper resources are allocated to ensure appropriate implementation. The following aspects of a methodology should be examined and taken into account:

✓ whether a service provider must be licensed or certified to implement the methodology;

✓ the initial training of service providers necessary to ensure proper implementation of the methodology;

✓ whether the methodology requires ongoing supervision by individuals with a particular license or certification, and at what intervals;

✓ whether the methodology calls for implementation in a particular setting (e.g., home, special education classroom, general education classroom);

✓ the equipment, if any, necessary to implement the methodology;

✓ any environmental variables that must be controlled to ensure proper implementation of the methodology;

✓ whether the methodology requires a specified staff-to-student ratio for proper implementation, since some methodologies call for staff-to-student ratios that are as low as one-to-one during initial implementation;

✓ whether the methodology prescribes the number of hours, days of the week, or days of the year for proper implementation;

✓ the data collection necessary to ensure proper implementation of the methodology, since many of the methodologies for children with autism spectrum disorders call for sophisticated data collection, record-keeping and analysis;

✓ the level of parental involvement necessary for proper implementation of the methodology;

✓ the ongoing support that service providers will need to enable implementation that maintains fidelity;

✓ the physical and mental effort required of service providers in order to implement the methodology, and the need to have trained back-up support; and

✓ the extent to which the methodology contemplates and permits flexibility to meet the unique needs of the individual child.

The focus of this book thus far has been on helping school districts understand and create the necessary structure for serving children with autism spectrum disorders. That structure consists of having a foundational understanding of the nature of autism (Chapter 2), designing and developing a comprehensive program (Chapter 3), and researching and selecting an array of sound methodologies to be implemented within a comprehensive program (Chapters 4 and 5). With this structure in place, we can turn our attention to the provision of a FAPE to an individual child, beginning with conducting a full and individual evaluation. The content of a child's IEP must be the result of a full individual evaluation. Chapter 6 discusses the role of such an evaluation in designing an IEP, including how the full and individual evaluation serves as a tool for selecting appropriate methodologies for implementing the child's IEP.

Chapter 6

Full and Individual Evaluation

Once a child is either suspected of having or identified as having an autism spectrum disorder and needing special education services, the district must bring all of its pre-planning and expertise to the table to evaluate the child, and if the child is determined eligible, to develop an individualized program for the child. The content of a child's IEP must be based on a full and individual evaluation of the child. The full and individual evaluation does more than determine eligibility — it informs and drives the development of the IEP.

The District Has the Right to Conduct Its Own Evaluation

Many children enter a school district already having been evaluated. Since the evaluation will drive both the program and range of appropriate methodologies, it is critical that the district conduct its own evaluation.

Even when the previous evaluation is current, the school district has the right to conduct its own evaluation. The district's well-established right in this regard is articulated by the non-autism-related case of *Andress v. Cleveland Independent School District*, 22 IDELR 1134, 64 F.3d 176 (5th Cir. 1995). That case involved a child, Wesley, who had been evaluated by the school district in 1982 and found to qualify for special education services under the IDEA as learning disabled and speech impaired.

Unfortunately, severe hazing by his high school classmates in spring 1987 caused Wesley to experience significant distress and precipitated his admission to a psychiatric hospital. A psychological evaluation conducted while he was in the hospital led to the following diagnosis:

> Gerstmann Syndrome, a condition which manifests itself through pronounced problems with social competency and indicates a high risk of developing psychopathology.[1]

Wesley's psychiatrist concluded that the boy's "condition was extremely aggravated by a phobia relating to school because of the hazing incident" and advised that he receive homebound instruction upon his release in May 1987, according to the district court case. Wesley's IEP team, which convened in August 1987, agreed, and the district provided homebound instruction for him during the 1987-1988 school year.

However, a dispute arose when the district informed Wesley's parents later that school year that his three-year reevaluation for special education eligibility and services was due in March 1988. The parents feared, based on medical advice from Wesley's psychiatrist, that the district's comprehensive reevaluation might precipitate a relapse for their son, and they refused consent for such a reevaluation. They also obtained independent evaluations; however, the district maintained that these were not acceptable as substitutes for its own reevaluation, without which it said that Wesley would no longer remain eligible for special education services. The parents then unilaterally enrolled Wesley in a private school, but continued to try to establish his special education eligibility through a series of private evaluations — each of which the school district rejected as insufficient to meet state criteria.

Wesley's parents filed a request for a due process hearing in December 1989 over this eligibility and evaluation dispute, and the hearing officer concluded that "the school district cannot be compelled to accept independent assessments in lieu of completing its own reevaluation." On appeal, the district court reversed the hearing officer's decision, finding that although a district generally has a right to conduct its own evaluation, an exception exists where such an evaluation would pose a risk of harm to the child's health. (*See Andress v. Cleveland Indep. Sch. Dist.*, 20 IDELR 743, 832 F. Supp. 1086 (E.D. Tex. 1993).)

However, the 5th Circuit Court of Appeals then reversed the district court's ruling on this issue:

> The district court erred in creating this judicial exception to the rule. The district court cited no law in support of its position. Nothing in the statutes, regulations or caselaw supports such an exception. Therefore, we hold that there is no exception to the rule that a school district has a right to test a student itself in order to evaluate or reevaluate the student's eligibility under IDEA.[2]

(*See also Marc V. b.n.f. Dr. Eugene V. v. North East Indep. Sch. Dist.*, 48 IDELR 41, 455 F. Supp. 2d 577 (W.D. Tex. 2006), *aff'd*, 242 Fed. Appx. 271 (5th Cir. 2007) (The court held that the district had the right to conduct its own evaluation and reevaluation of the child's eligibility under the IDEA, and was not required to consent to the homebound placement requested by the parent when the parent refused to consent to the IEP team's request to discuss the placement recommendation with the child's physician.); *M.T.V. v. DeKalb County Sch. Dist.*, 45 IDELR 177, 446 F.3d 1153 (11th Cir. 2006) (The court upheld the district's right to condition the child's continued special education services on a re-evaluation by an expert of its choosing.); *Patricia P. v. Board of Educ. of Oak Park*, 31 IDELR 211, 203 F.3d 462, 469 (7th Cir. 2000) (The court held that "parents who, because of their failure to cooperate, do not allow a school district a reasonable opportunity to evaluate their disabled child, forfeit their claim for reimbursement for a unilateral private placement."); and *Schwartz v. The Learning Center Academy*, 34 IDELR 3 (W.D. Mich. 2001) (The court concluded that the parent's failure to allow the district to conduct a Section 504-eligibility evaluation of a child precluded a challenge of discrimination under that statute).)

Children Transitioning from IDEA Part C to IDEA Part B Services

Some children are identified, evaluated, and have been receiving services through an IDEA Part C early childhood program before coming to the attention of school officials. Sometimes a methodology dispute arises because the parent wants the school district to use the same methodology that was used in (or funded by) the Part C program.

This situation arose in *Steinmetz v. Richmond Community School Corp.*, 33 IDELR 155 (S.D. Ind. 2000). In that case, Andrew was diagnosed as having autism at 22 months. He was referred to Indiana's First Steps Program, where he was evaluated and determined to have notable deficiencies in his language and fine motor skills. An IFSP was developed for him; however, after 10 weeks, Andrew's parents withdrew him from the early childhood program because they were dissatisfied with its services. Instead, the parents "instituted a program of [ABA] facilitated by the Rutgers Autism Program" for Andrew. The Rutgers program consisted of daily one-on-one sessions, which increased from 20 hours per week to 40 hours per week in a little over a year. Although this program of ABA methodology was initially

> developed without regard to the IFSP that had been developed by the First Steps Program and without any direct contact between Rutgers and First Steps . . . [a] portion of the ABA program was funded by First Steps until April 15, 1998, when Andrew turned three years old and the [school district] became involved with providing Andrew's special education and related services.

Over the course of multiple IEP team meetings in spring and summer of 1998, the parents sought to have the district's IEP continue the provision of intensive at-home ABA services for Andrew. District personnel evaluated Andrew following a March 1998 transition conference with the parents, and thereafter proposed an IEP that did not contain the desired services. The parents responded with a written statement, which included the following:

> [Andrew] has undergone multiple evaluations by [district] personnel . . . and in general, we agree with the results of these evaluations. He is diagnosed with autism and presents with deficits in communication, socialization, and self-help skills as well as sensory defensiveness.
>
> Currently through the First Steps Program, Andrew is undergoing an eclectic therapy that includes Speech and Occupational (Sensory Integration) Therapy as well as an intensive in-home behavioral [ABA] program. We agree with the self-help issues but feel that the IEP does not include key elements found in his current program that are leading to great progress in a variety of areas. For many reasons, continuing Andrew's current plan as outlined in his IFSP is the most appropriate placement for Andrew.

The district's April 1998 IEP incorporated a "transition period" from April 15 to June 3, with services designed to prepare Andrew for entry into a community preschool. The parents agreed with the plan for such placement "assuming that his social and attending skills have increased to the point where he can receive benefit from this placement," but the record indicates that Andrew did not participate in this program, the court said.

At a subsequent meeting in July 1998, the IEP team considered and revised the April IEP to include a range of services including:

> training for those providing services [for] Andrew, including training concerning a picture exchange system, intervention techniques particularly concerning behavioral and comforting issues, positive reinforcement techniques, sensory integration techniques and techniques involving ABA methodology.

The parents rejected this IEP. Shortly thereafter, they requested a due process hearing seeking reimbursement for Andrew's program of ABA methodology and alleging that the district's IEP did not offer him a FAPE. The due process hearing officer found that the district's program was "appropriate and reasonably calculated" to provide a FAPE, and that therefore the parents were not entitled to be reimbursed for "costs they incurred in the unilateral placement" of Andrew in a program of ABA methodology. This decision was affirmed by an appeals board, and subsequently by a federal district court. In support of its ruling, the court noted that the school district's proposed July 1998 IEP contained a detailed program of services. The IEP also incorporated a detailed transition plan to help Andrew adjust from his at-home program to the pre-school placement. The court went on to make specific findings regarding the appropriateness of the district's evaluation and its reliance on that evaluation in designing a program of services for Andrew:

> Prior to the time of Andrew's evaluations, the [district] created an Autism Team which consisted of a group of education professionals who participated in a six-day training at the Institute for the Study of Developmental Disability at IU in Bloomington and other training programs. . . . Members of the team which evaluated Andrew and put together his IEP were: [ ], Ph.D., a school psychologist, [ ], M.A., Assistant Director of Special Education for the School, [ ], M.A., an Early Childhood Special Education Teacher currently teaching preschool although previously she taught children with moderate and severe disabilities in middle school, [ ], M.A., [occupational therapist]

for the [district], who tested Andrew and was scheduled to deliver OT services to him, [ ], M.A., [speech language pathologist], and [ ], M.A., Director of Special Education for the [district].

In general, the members of the team testified that they were familiar with and recommended a wide variety of methodologies for specific students with autism depending on the needs of individual students. . . . The team members had substantial classroom and private experience with children with autism . . .

. . . Many members of the assembled team had observed Andrew in his home during his training time, spoke to his Parents, and also tested Andrew according to their specialty. The multi-disciplinary team produced an evaluation report as a starting point to formulate an effective IEP for Andrew. In addition, it is noteworthy to point out that although the [district] did not follow the lead of the Parents in choosing an education modality for Andrew, the July IEP and subsequent action plan included training and education in the ABA methodology for those provided [sic] services to Andrew.

. . .

. . . Although the Parents have successfully demonstrated that the [district's] plans do not adhere to the methodology they prefer, they have not demonstrated that the School failed to take Andrew's unique needs into consideration.

. . .

The record before this court supports a finding by this court that the July IEP is adequate and appropriate to ensure the requisite degree of educational benefit to Andrew.

The IDEA requires that "[c]hildren participating in early intervention programs assisted under [IDEA Part C], and who will participate in preschool programs assisted [under IDEA Part B], experience a smooth and effective transition to those preschool programs. . . ." 20 USC 1412(a)(9). With respect to transition, the lead agency for the IDEA Part C services must:

(I) notify the local educational agency for the area in which such a child resides that the child will shortly reach the age of eligibility for preschool services under subchapter II, as determined in accordance with State law;

(II) in the case of a child who may be eligible for such preschool services, with the approval of the family of the child, convene a conference among the lead agency, the family, and the local educational agency not less than 90 days (and at the discretion of all such parties, not more than 9 months) before the child is eligible for the preschool services, to discuss any such services that the child may receive; and

(III) in the case of a child who may not be eligible for such preschool services, with the approval of the family, make reasonable efforts to convene a conference among the lead agency, the family, and providers of other appropriate services for children who are not eligible for preschool services under subchapter II, to discuss the appropriate services that the child may receive. . . .

20 USC 1437(a)(9)(A)(ii).

The school district should use the 90-day conference to acquire as much information about the child as possible so that the district can design its evaluation plan. The district should not automatically replicate services provided or funded via the IFSP or substitute the Part C evaluation for its own evaluation. The district should wisely use this 90-day period to complete its evaluation and make a determination of eligibility. If the child is determined eligible for IDEA Part B special education and related services, the district is required to ensure that "[b]y the third birthday of such a child, an individualized education program or . . . an individualized family service plan, has been developed and is being implemented for the child." 20 USC 1412(a)(9).

Children Entering the District from a Private School Program, Including a Home-Based Program

Some children are identified, evaluated, and have been receiving services in a private school program, including a home-based program. If the child is coming from a private program with an existing evaluation that proposes a program or methodology that the parent wants the public school to implement, the parent will often be reluctant to allow the district to conduct its own evaluation.

In the case of *E.W. by C.W. v. Rocklin Unified School District*, 46 IDELR 192 (E.D. Cal. 2006), the school district insisted on its right to conduct its own evaluation after the child enrolled in the district from a home-based Lovaas program. E.W. was 3 years old when his parents began meeting with representatives of the Rocklin Unified School District to develop an IEP. He was receiving private ABA services from the Lovaas Institute of Early Intervention and his parents requested that the school fund the home-based program. In September 2003, the district initially offered to place him in a program designed for children with autism for a 30-day transition period (to "permit the development of a longer-term FAPE"), and at an April 2004 IEP team meeting, the district developed and proposed an evaluation plan recommending that E.W. be evaluated in academic, cognitive, communication, motor, health, social/emotional, and pre-vocational areas. The parents refused to consent to the evaluation plan and requested a due process hearing on this and other issues. The parents believed that the district should have used data from E.W.'s private home-based program to determine that he should continue in the home-based ABA program at public expense.

The hearing officer found that the district had a right to conduct its own full and individual evaluation. The district's proposed evaluation was necessary to provide E.W. with an appropriate education, but the district had been denied any opportunity to perform its evaluation. The hearing officer also noted that the evaluation used in the home-based program was not as comprehensive as the evaluation proposed by the district.

The parents appealed to district court, but the court agreed with the hearing officer that the district had the right to complete its own full and individual evaluation. "[T]he Ninth Circuit [has] stated that 'if parents want [their child] to receive special education under the Act, they are obligated to permit such testing.'" (*E.W. by C.W. quoting Gregory K. v. Longview Sch. Dist.*, 558 IDELR 284 (EHLR 558:284), 811 F.2d 1307, 1315 (9th Cir. 1987).)

Districts should be mindful when conducting the evaluation that the parents may be planning to ask the district to pay for the private school placement without regard to whether the public school has had an opportunity to educate the child. The case of *Board of Education of the City School District of the City of New York v. Tom F.*, 106 LRP 48499, 193 Fed. Appx. 26 (2d Cir. 2006), *aff'd per curiam*, 48 IDELR 239 (2007), provides an example of one parent who won continued public funding for a private school placement even though the child had never attended the public school in question.

Gilbert, the son of Tom F., had attended a private school since kindergarten, in 1995. The district initially evaluated him in 1996 and paid the private school tuition for the 1997-1998 and 1998-1999 school years. In 1999, the district conducted Gilbert's annual review and proposed an IEP that would provide Gilbert with special education services in a public school classroom with a student-to-teacher ratio of 15:1. Tom F. rejected the proposed IEP, continued Gilbert's enrollment at the private school, and requested a due process hearing to demand reimbursement for private school. The hearing officer and a state review officer both ruled in favor of the parent, concluding that the district had denied Gilbert a FAPE because the child's special education teacher had been absent from the annual review.

The district court then reversed the administrative rulings, holding that the parents of a child who had never attended a public school could not receive reimbursement for private school tuition under the IDEA. (*See Board of Educ. of the City Sch. Dist. of New York v. Tom F. ex rel. Gilbert F.*, 42 IDELR 171 (S.D.N.Y. 2005).)[3]

However, on appeal, the 2d Circuit Court of Appeals vacated the district court's decision and returned the case to the lower court, ordering it to apply the law as the 2d Circuit recently had explained it in a similar case awarding private school reimbursement to the parents of a child who had never attended public school.[4] The U.S. Supreme Court later affirmed the 2d Circuit's ruling in a 4-4 decision in 2007 (in which Justice Kennedy did not take part). This split decision means that, although the 2d Circuit's ruling in the parent's favor in the *Tom F.* case remains in place, the issue of whether a child must be enrolled in a public school district before parents may obtain reimbursement for private school remains unresolved among the Circuit Courts. So depending on which circuit is involved, a parent of a child with a disability may or may not be barred from seeking reimbursement for a private school program, including a home-based program, if the child has never attended the public school district.

With this in mind, school districts should conduct each full and individual evaluation using multiple evaluation tools in multiple settings, including in the private school or any home-based program setting. The case of *Michael J. v. Derry Township School District*, 45 IDELR 36 (M.D. Pa. 2006), is a nice example of an effective evaluation of a child who was in a private home-based program at the time the school district conducted its evaluation. Patrick J. began a home-based program of ABA methodology when he was 3 years old. When Patrick was 6, his parents began meeting with district representatives to develop an appropriate public school program for him. The district requested and was granted permission to conduct a full and individual evaluation. A district occupational therapist observed Patrick at his preschool, noting that he roamed the room, made little eye contact, and circled the perimeter of the playground. He also attempted some parallel play, responded to certain environmental cues, and answered some direct questions. His fine and gross motor skills appeared to be sufficiently developed for his age. A school psychologist administered the Stanford-Binet Intelligence Scale 4th Edition, the Woodcock Reading Mastery Test, and the Bracken Basic Concept Scale-Revised. A district speech and language pathologist administered the Peabody Picture Vocabulary Test, the Expressive One Word Picture Vocabulary Test, and the Preschool Language Scale. These were used to test both auditory comprehension and expressive communication. The school psychologist summarized the results of these assessments when she wrote that Patrick "'was noted to have severe receptive, expressive, and pragmatic language delay with need for intensive speech and language services in his school program.'" The district shared a copy of the report with the parents.

At the initial IEP team meeting, the district and the parents discussed Patrick's present levels of educational performance, strengths, and needs. The IEP team made decisions regarding annual goals, short-term objectives, and specially designed instruction. The district offered Patrick instruction using TEACCH strategies, ABA, one-to-one instruction, small group instruction and repeated practice. However, Mr. and Mrs. J. felt that Patrick's educational needs would be better addressed at a private school they were attempting to open. The private school would use ABA as the primary methodology. After encountering some difficulty in opening their school, they proposed that the district fund a significant portion of Patrick's home-based program until the school opened. The J.'s and the district continued to communicate about the situation through letters and attorneys. District representatives observed Patrick in the home-based program. Eventually, discussions between the parents and the district broke down. Patrick's parents continued their private home-based program for Patrick without district funding.

Later, the J.'s enrolled Patrick in their newly opened school. They requested a due process hearing to compel the district to reimburse them for enrollment costs. The hearing was decided in favor of the district. After receiving a second judgment against them before a state appeals panel, the parents took the case to district court. They claimed that the evaluations completed by the school district were inadequate. However, the court determined that the district's evaluation had been sufficient:

> Substantial evidence in the record supports a finding that the goals and objectives contained in Patrick's IEP were based upon consideration of information the IEP team derived from numerous sources, including psychiatric evaluations, educational assessments, parental input, and observation of Patrick's then-current placement.

As the *Michael J.* case illustrates, in a methodology dispute, an evaluation that includes observations of the child in the child's private school program, including a home-based program, is extremely valuable. This is particularly true when the child can be observed using the parent's preferred methodology. Such an observation will assist the district in evaluating the parent's request for a particular methodology and the parent's representations as to the level of success their child has experienced using such methodology. Whether the child can receive an educational benefit using another methodology is also something that can be evaluated through observations of the child in his or her private school program including a home-based program.

Children Transferring from Other Public School Districts

Some children transfer from other public school districts. The regulations implementing the IDEA 2004 requirements address both in-state and out-of-state transfers as follows:

> If a child with a disability (who had an IEP that was in effect in a previous public agency in the same State) transfers to a new public agency in the same State, and enrolls in a new school within the same school year, the new public agency (in consultation with the parents) must provide FAPE to the child (including services comparable to those described in the child's IEP from the previous public agency), until the new public agency either —
>
> (1) Adopts the child's IEP from the previous public agency; or
>
> (2) Develops, adopts, and implements a new IEP that meets the applicable requirements in §§300.320 through 300.324.

34 CFR 300.323(e).

> If a child with a disability (who had an IEP that was in effect in a previous public agency in another State) transfers to a public agency in a new State, and enrolls in a new school within the same school year, the new public agency (in consultation with the parents) must provide the child with FAPE (including services comparable to those described in the child's IEP from the previous public agency), until the new public agency —
>
> (1) Conducts an evaluation pursuant to §§300.304 through 300.306 (if determined to be necessary by the new public agency); and

(2) Develops, adopts, and implements a new IEP, if appropriate, that meets the applicable requirements in §§300.320 through 300.324.

34 CFR 300.323(f).

The regulations do not require a receiving school district to conduct a reevaluation when a child has been identified and served in another public school. Often there is a need to reevaluate when the child is transferring from an out-of-state public school because eligibility criteria are often different from state to state.

Whether or not eligibility is at issue, the district's ability to conduct effective individualized program planning may be compromised when the district does not conduct its own evaluation.

Sometimes the evaluation may be in the form of an interim IEP and diagnostic placement. The case of *Lt. T.B. ex rel. N.B. v. Warwick School Committee*, 40 IDELR 253, 361 F.3d 80 (1st Cir. 2004), illustrates such an approach. The family moved to Warwick, Rhode Island after being reassigned by the Navy from Georgia. Before moving, the parents contacted the Warwick school district to learn what services would be available for their son N.B., who had autism. They also delivered a packet of materials containing expert evaluations of N.B., which had been completed within the last year in Georgia. The district organized an IEP team meeting two days after the family's arrival. They attempted to schedule a time to meet N.B. before the IEP team meeting, but Mrs. B. did not receive the request in time for that to occur. Using the materials provided by the parents, the district then proposed an interim IEP that would allow for evaluation of N.B.'s performance for one month. N.B. would be placed in a self-contained classroom in which TEACCH methodologies would be used. His parents rejected the IEP and enrolled N.B. in a private school that used Discrete Trial Training (DTT) methodology. They also requested a due process hearing and asked the district to pay for the private placement. The hearing officer ruled that the district lacked sufficient knowledge regarding N.B. to choose a methodology other than DTT. He ordered the district to pay the costs of N.B.'s tuition at the private school.

Mr. and Mrs. B. went to federal district court seeking attorney's fees and costs, while the school district counterclaimed to challenge the findings of the hearing officer. The court ruled that the school district's IEP did not deny N.B. a FAPE, and the B.'s claim for attorney's fees was dismissed. The parents subsequently appealed to the 1st Circuit Court of Appeals. There, they argued that the school district had not completed an appropriate evaluation of N.B. prior to developing his IEP, because no one from the district had met their son, nor did they have his complete records. The court disagreed. First, the court applied the relevant section of the IDEA to determine that there is no rule requiring that district representatives meet with a child before preparing an IEP:

> IDEA regulations require that the team members be "knowledgeable about the child, the meaning of the evaluation data, and the placement options." Whether the team must meet the child to perform an evaluation surely depends on the situation, particularly the availability of other information. There is no per se rule that unless the child is seen and heard by the team, the procedures for preparing an IEP have been violated.

The court then explained that the district had complied with the procedures outlined within the IDEA by using the information available at the time to create an interim IEP, which would allow the district to consider the results of its own diagnostic placement:

> Warwick reviewed all the records available at the time, met with Mrs. B. for six hours over two different days (April 13 and May 4), and assembled a team with considerable expertise in autism. The team read the prior evaluations of N.B., along with additional evaluation materials provided by Mrs. B. at the April 13 meeting, and heard from his mother and her special education lawyer about various educational techniques that N.B. had tried. The record also supports Warwick's contention that the IEP proposed

on April 13 was an interim one, which would be reviewed one month later, after Warwick could study how N.B. responded to it.

When considering the *Warwick* case, it is important to keep in mind that the dispute arose before the IDEA 2004 provisions concerning transfer students were in effect. Therefore, we do not know whether the result would have been the same under the IDEA 2004. As previously stated, for both in-state and out-of-state transfer students, the IDEA and its implementing regulations now require "the new public agency (in consultation with the parents) . . . [to] provide FAPE to the child (including services comparable to those described in the child's IEP from the previous public agency). . . ." 34 CFR 300.323(e)-(f). In a methodology dispute such as the *Warwick* case, the outcome of the case may turn on the interpretation of the term "comparable" services. If the district is given the opportunity to implement an interim IEP and diagnostic placement before litigation ensues, the resulting functional evaluation data can be extremely beneficial in any subsequent litigation. The data from such a placement should be thoughtfully gathered and analyzed.

How Evaluation Drives Decision-Making

Evaluation is about more than determining eligibility. Evaluation drives the decisions about the child's program of services, including the range of appropriate methodologies. The full and individual evaluation must assist in determining "[t]he content of the child's IEP." 34 CFR 300.304(b)(1)(ii). The full and individual evaluation must be

> sufficiently comprehensive to identify all of the child's special education and related services needs, whether or not commonly linked to the disability category in which the child has been classified.

34 CFR 300.304(c)(6).

> [It must include] [a]ssessment tools and strategies that provide relevant information that directly assists persons in determining the educational needs of the child. . . .

34 CFR 300.304(c)(7).

When conducting an evaluation under the IDEA, the child must be assessed by "trained and knowledgeable personnel." 34 CFR 300.304(c)(1)(iv). In order to conduct an evaluation and produce an evaluation report that will provide the basis for programming and methodology decisions, the team of professionals should be knowledgeable about: (1) the nature of autism spectrum disorders; (2) the research regarding essential components of an effective program for children with autism spectrum disorders; (3) the peer-reviewed research-based instructional methodologies for children with autism spectrum disorders; and (4) the theories underlying each of the methodologies currently being utilized in the district, including the specific needs these methodologies are designed to address.

Courts are influenced by evidence of how well a district uses its full and individual evaluation to make programming decisions, including its decisions regarding instructional methodology. The case of *J.P. ex rel. Popson v. West Clark Community Schools*, 38 IDELR 5, 230 F. Supp. 2d 910 (S.D. Ind. 2002), discussed earlier, illustrates how an evaluation should drive individual programming decisions. When J.P. was found eligible for special education services, West Clark Community Schools completed a full and individual evaluation to identify his educational needs as a child with autism. The district then used that information to drive its decisions regarding goal development, programming (including methodology selection), and placement. Evaluation results revealed the following about J.P.:

[He] (1) was not yet toilet trained; (2) did not engage in appropriate play or use common gestures; (3) was significantly below average in intellectual and cognitive functions; (4) was mildly deficient in adaptive functioning; (5) was not able to imitate adult sounds, use gestures to make his needs known, or raise his arms in response to commands such as "up" or "come here," (6) was not able to use any words, though he did know the meaning of a few words; and (7) was not able to listen to or follow instructions requiring an action and an object.

Furthermore, his expressive language skills were rated at the level of 4 to 8 months, and his receptive communication skills in the 8-to-16 month old age range. His fine and gross motor skills were delayed. He did not combine vocalization with non-verbal gestures or body movements.

The evaluation was deemed by the court to be sufficiently specific to provide the basis for programming decisions. The court explained:

As a result of the evaluation, [the district] recommended that J.P. would benefit from continued participation in an early childhood environment that provides him with frequent opportunities to interact with peers, as well as with adults, and to use a wide variety of manipulative materials. According to West Clark's report, J.P.'s educational program should provide consistent routines, with ample preparation for any changes in routine, an opportunity for structured social interchanges, an opportunity to learn a functional communication system, and consistent reinforcement of desired behaviors. The report also stated that [J.P.] needed to be encouraged to attend to individuals and tasks by making good eye contact and that he would require speech therapy to address his functional communication difficulties.

The evaluation further provided the basis for rejecting the parent's preferred methodology and placement options. "The [district] explicitly rejected other options, such as home-based education, education through a separate private facility, and education through a public residential facility." Instead,

J.P.'s initial IEP called for him to be placed in a preschool program with special education assistance for 12.5 hours per week. This included 80 minutes per week of speech therapy and 120 minutes per week of occupational therapy. The IEP further required that a teacher's aide be available to assist J.P.

After he began attending the public school, the district continued to evaluate J.P.'s performance to obtain information for further decision-making regarding goals, methods, and placement. The IEP team later developed new goals based on evaluations conducted during the time he attended school. The district recommended that J.P.'s needs should continue to be addressed through the full-time placement provided by the district.

The Popsons believed that J.P. would be better educated through the use of a strict ABA/DTT methodology similar to that described by Ivar Lovaas. They were not satisfied with the district's offer of an "eclectic" program using ABA/DTT, PECS, and small-group instruction. The parents requested a due process hearing to challenge the district's methodology decisions. However, the district's decisions were upheld by the hearing officer and by subsequent rulings of the Board of Special Education Appeals and the federal district court.

The court recognized that the school district's instructional methodology decisions were based on evaluation data and were appropriately designed to address J.P.'s unique educational needs, especially in the area of functional communication and social skills development, to help prepare him for eventual placement in a regular classroom, as follows:

The greater care that West Clark took in developing J.P.'s IEPs is indicative of the fact that West Clark's special education teachers had a greater understanding of J.P.'s needs [than did educators in another case used by the court for comparison]. . . . As J.P.'s classroom teacher testified, these techniques included PECS and one-on-one ABA/DTT training, as well as group time designed to bring J.P. into the general preschool program.

The court concluded that the district had used proper procedures to develop "a program for J.P. that was reasonably calculated to provide him with meaningful educational benefits." (*See also W.S. ex rel. C.S. v. Rye City Sch. Dist.,* 46 IDELR 285, 454 F. Supp. 2d 134 (S.D.N.Y. 2006) (The court upheld the appropriateness of the district's IEP where, in developing and modifying the IEP, the district considered both the results of its own thorough triennial reevaluation as well as "substantial additional testing" obtained by the parent.).)

The district must "[u]se a variety of assessment tools and strategies to gather relevant functional, developmental, and academic information about the child, including information provided by the parent. . . ." 34 CFR 300.304(b)(1).

Any information that the parent may have should be fully explored by the evaluation team as part of the full and individual evaluation to determine the instructional implications. If, for example, the parent has utilized a home-based program, the evaluation team should request and carefully consider any information the parent provides regarding the program itself, as well as any data the parent has collected about the child's progress as part of the home-based program. In *County School Board of Henrico County, VA v. R.T.,* 45 IDELR 274, 433 F. Supp. 2d 657 (E.D. Va. 2006), the district failed during its evaluation process to consider information provided by the parent — a decision that contributed to the court's ruling in the parent's favor.

While RT's mother, concerned about her son's perceived lack of progress in the district's preschool program, sought to have him admitted to the district's elementary school autism program at Twin Hickory, she also

> began intensively researching ABA therapy. In the spring of 2002, she endeavored to design a home ABA program for her son. Mrs. T. enlisted the assistance of Amanda Adkins, a 2002 graduate of the University of Virginia who had spent two years during college and one year after college doing in-home ABA therapy to develop and implement an in-home ABA program. The two women conducted the program in RT's home during the summer of 2002.

> In September 2002, an IEP team convened to design an IEP for RT's education at Twin Hickory. . . . At [that] IEP meeting, *Mrs. T. presented research that she had done on ABA therapy, outlined the progress that she believed RT had made under that mode of instruction over the summer, and requested that ABA therapy be included in the IEP.* The September IEP noted that request, but rejected it with the comment that RT was going to be continued using his existing IEP goals under the TEACCH program at Twin Hickory until a reevaluation of his present level of performance could be accomplished. (Emphasis added.)

Following that meeting, "both the parents and the [district] conducted evaluations of RT," and then reconvened two successive IEP team meetings (one in October and one in November).

When, as discussed in previous chapters, the parents challenged the district's proposed IEP in a due process hearing and in court, the district defended its IEP by arguing that its appropriateness needed to be gauged in relation to RT's potential — and that his progress using the TEACCH methodology was appropriate because he lacked the cognitive capacity to make more progress than he had. However, the court concluded that the district "was not correct in its assessment that RT had made and could make adequate progress in the TEACCH program." The court found that the district had "greatly misunderstood RT's cognitive capacity and educational needs," and that its proposed IEP "both underestimated and inappropriately served him." This result suggests that, had the school district given genuine consideration to the information and data supplied by the parent, and used its own evaluation data to assess the parent's information, the outcome might have been different. The court stated:

> [T]he preponderance of the evidence demonstrated that to [progress in key areas of need], RT required a highly structured, highly focused education methodology such as ABA therapy in which RT would receive intensive one-on-one instruction. The TEACCH program at Twin Hickory was not designed to, and did not, and could not provide RT with this type of instruction. *And, in the fall of 2002, the [district] understood that fact.* (Emphasis added.)

The development of an individually tailored program, including methodologies that are reasonably calculated to enable the child to receive an educational benefit, begin with a well-planned and well-executed full and individual evaluation. Given the importance of an individual evaluation for a child with an autism spectrum disorder in designing a program that includes appropriate methodologies, districts should not give up their right to evaluate, or pass up the opportunity to comprehensively evaluate. As part of its evaluation, the district can and should carefully examine whether its existing programs and methodologies are appropriate for the particular child being evaluated. The predetermination identified in Chapter 4 as problematic can be avoided with a comprehensive evaluation that examines an array of methodologies that may be appropriate for the individual child. A district should not retreat from the opportunity to include as part of its evaluation an examination of the methodology or methodologies preferred by the parent, particularly when the child already has been receiving services that include the parent's preferred methodology. With a full and individual evaluation in place, the district is ready to conduct an IEP team meeting. Chapter 7 guides school districts through the next steps of preparing for and conducting an IEP team meeting.

ENDNOTES

[1] *Andress v. Cleveland Indep. Sch. Dist.,* 20 IDELR 743, 832 F. Supp. 1086, 1088 (E.D. Tex. 1993).

[2] *Andress v. Cleveland Indep. Sch. Dist.,* 22 IDELR 1134, 64 F.3d at 176 (5th Cir. 1995).

[3] The court's analysis focused on the then-current IDEA regulation at 34 CFR 300.403(c) (now in its revised version at 34 CFR 300.148(c)), which authorizes reimbursement for private school to parents of a child with a disability "who previously received special education and related services" from a public school district, if the district failed to provide FAPE to the child.

[4] *See Frank G. v. Board of Educ. of Hyde Park,* 46 IDELR 33, 459 F.3d 356 (2d Cir. 2006), *cert. denied,* 128 S. Ct. 436 (2007) (Where school district acknowledged its failure to provide FAPE, the court held that it was consistent with the purpose of the IDEA to award reimbursement for private school rather than forcing the child to first endure inappropriate public school services in order to qualify for such reimbursement.).

Chapter 7

IEP Team Meetings

Preparation versus Predetermination

The IDEA affords parents the opportunity to participate in "meetings" under the Act. The regulations specify this right as follows:

> Parent participation in meetings.
>
> (1) The parents of a child with a disability must be afforded an opportunity to participate in meetings with respect to —
>
>> (i) The identification, evaluation, and educational placement of the child; and
>>
>> (ii) The provision of FAPE to the child.
>
> (2) Each public agency must provide notice consistent with §300.322(a)(1) and (b)(1) to ensure that parents of children with disabilities have the opportunity to participate in meetings described in paragraph (b)(1) of this section.

34 CFR 300.501(b)(1)-(2).

The regulations further contemplate the need by districts to participate in preparatory activities prior to an IEP team meeting, and, accordingly, permit school districts to engage in such preparatory activities without the parent's participation:

> A meeting does not include informal or unscheduled conversations involving public agency personnel and conversations on issues such as teaching methodology, lesson plans, or coordination of service provision. A meeting also does not include preparatory activities that public agency personnel engage in to develop a proposal or response to a parent proposal that will be discussed at a later meeting.

34 CFR 300.501(b)(3).

Nevertheless, school districts must be careful to ensure that planning and preparation do not result in predetermination. The USDE in its discussion of the regulations discourages the development of draft IEPs that may have the effect of precluding parent participation on the IEP team:

> We do not encourage public agencies to prepare a draft IEP prior to the IEP Team meeting, particularly if doing so would inhibit a full discussion of the child's needs. However, if a public agency develops a draft IEP prior to the IEP Team meeting, the agency should make it clear to the parents at the outset of the meeting that the services proposed by the agency are preliminary recommendations for review and discussion with the parents. The public agency also should provide the parents with a copy of its draft proposals, if the agency has developed them, prior to the IEP Team meeting so as to give the parents an opportunity to review the recommendations of the public agency

prior to the IEP Team meeting, and be better able to engage in a full discussion of the proposals for the IEP.

71 Fed. Reg. 46,678 (2006).

The courts are seemingly more tolerant of draft IEPs. In *Grant by Sunderlin v. Independent School District No. 11, Anoka-Hennepin*, 43 IDELR 219 (D. Minn. 2005), the court stated, "[n]either the IDEA nor its regulations prohibit a District from coming to an IEP meeting with suggestions to facilitate the development of a proposed IEP." The court was persuaded by the evidence that the document at issue in this case was a genuine draft for parent input, and not an indication of predetermination:

> Ryberg, the Student's case manager, testified that, consistent with the school's practice, she explained the document was a "draft" when she distributed it at the start of the meeting. During the meeting Ryberg consistently referred to the document as a draft. . . . In [the parents' presence], Ryberg wrote "Draft" across the top corner of each page. [The parents'] copy also includes the words "rough draft" on the second page, words which the Student's stepfather testified suggest the document was not the final IEP. Based on this evidence, the Court concludes . . . the January 31, 2001 document was a "draft" IEP.

(*See also J.D. v. Kanawha County Bd. of Educ.*, 48 IDELR 159 (S.D. W. Va. 2007) (The court held that the existence of draft IEP does not, by itself, show predetermination: "'[I]f there were evidence that a school district had been inflexible and refused changes to a draft IEP,' then this would be evidence toward predetermination. Here, however, the Board accepted many of the parents' suggestions. The school system's choice not to include the suggested services that the parents proposed does not mean that the IEP was predetermined."); *Michael J. v. Derry Township School Dist.*, 45 IDELR 36 (M.D. Pa. 2006) (Evidence that the district had created "Notice of Recommended Educational Placement" prior to the IEP meeting did not, by itself, establish evidence of predetermination, especially in light of the "full-day IEP meeting" and "ample evidence . . . that [district personnel] . . . were engaging in a good faith evaluation of an appropriate educational placement for" the student.); *E.W. by C.W. v. Rocklin Unified Sch. Dist.*, 46 IDELR 192 (E.D. Cal. 2006) ("School officials are permitted to form . . . opinions and compile reports prior to the IEP meetings, as long as a meaningful IEP meeting is subsequently conducted where various options are discussed and considered. . . . [T]he discussion section of the [IEP] is replete with references to input provided by [the] parents."); *Board of Educ. of Township High Sch. Dist. No. 211 v. Michael R. and Diane R. ex rel. Lindsey R.*, 44 IDELR 36 (N.D. Ill. 2005) (The school district's preparation for an IEP meeting did not rise to the level of predetermination, as evidence demonstrated that district personnel listened to and considered parents' proposals at the meeting: "[S]chool districts are permitted to prepare for IEP meetings, including drafting proposals and thinking about the appropriate placement recommendation. . . . School officials must come to the IEP table with an open mind, but they need not come with a blank mind.").)

Clearly, whether or not a school district's preparation for an IEP team meeting constitutes predetermination is a very fact-specific question. The case of *T.P. and S.P., on behalf of S.P. v. Mamaroneck Union Free School District*, 47 IDELR 287 (S.D.N.Y. 2007), in terms of both the facts and the outcome, stands in contrast to the cases upholding the preparation of a draft IEP. S.P. was diagnosed at age 2 as having PDD-NOS, and at age 4 as having "an auditory processing disorder, fine and gross motor delays and an expressive language disorder." The district identified him for IDEA purposes as a child with autism.

S.P. received 40 hours of ABA methodology in his preschool year, as well as speech and occupational therapies. The following year (2003-2004), the parents and the district disagreed over the district's recommended IEP, which did not include intensive ABA methodology. Ultimately, however, the parents and the district entered into a settlement agreement that resulted in the provision to S.P. of continued intensive ABA methodology at home as well as "speech therapy four times per week[ ] and occupational therapy two times per week." He also "attended a regular education preschool class with a full time 1:1 behaviorally trained teacher for 10 hours per week."

In May and June of 2004, the private center that had originally diagnosed S.P. reevaluated him and recommended continued home-based ABA 1:1 services at least 25 hours per week, as well as "individual speech-language therapy five times per week; individual occupational therapy five times per week; and enrollment in a structured, language-based special education kindergarten class with a behaviorally trained aide and low student to teacher ratio."

The district also evaluated S.P. during this time, and concluded in pertinent part that he "did not need the intensive instructional services typically provided to children with autism." As a result, the district's proposed IEP in June 2004 consisted of "placement in a 12:1+2 special class; 30 minutes of group speech therapy three times per week; 30 minutes of individual OT two times per week; [and] 30 minutes of individual speech therapy one time per week. . . ."

A second meeting was convened in July 2004, at which time the parents presented the private evaluator's report for consideration by the IEP team, raised concerns about the district's proposal and made specific requests for certain, more intensive services for their son.

Despite this, the IEP that the district ultimately proposed in September 2004 was largely unchanged from the one that it had presented to the parents at the June 2004 meeting. The parents filed a request for a due process hearing, alleging among other things that the July 2004 meeting had been a "sham" and that the district had "impermissibly predetermined what services [S.P.] would receive at a private meeting without the child's parents present, conducted just minutes before the start of the July . . . meeting." Both the due process hearing officer and a state review officer upheld the appropriateness of the school district's IEP, and the parents took the case to federal court.

The court considered evidence that the district's ABA supervisor and autism consultant had prepared "a comparative chart or note of sorts . . . just moments before the July [IEP] meeting, which [the ABA supervisor] curiously did not attend." The court described the chart as follows:

> This handwritten document lists in column-style comparison format the treatment and support [recommended by the parents' private evaluator] and next to those, the [district's recommendations].

There were sharp differences between several of the key recommendations presented by the parents and those from the district (e.g., "where [the private evaluator] recommended 25 hours of ABA at home . . . the school responsibility was listed as 10 hours in school. . . .").

The court's Memorandum Opinion contains the following analysis of the school district's conduct:

> While [the ABA supervisor] attended the June IEP meeting . . . she did not attend the July IEP meeting, as she felt she had "already written everything that [she] needed to present." This presumably includes the side by side comparison chart prepared just before the meeting on July 16. . . . She also testified that prior to the July meeting, she met with [district personnel] "to talk about appropriate placement options and to look at staffing patterns and building different programs in different buildings to see what would be appropriate placement and staffing and training needs" and responded "yes," when asked whether [S.P.'s] name came up at that meeting.
>
> The services listed on the comparative list prior to commencement of the July IEP meeting, are just the services that the District ultimately provided, despite the Parents' protests and request for some at-home ABA services. . . . While the Court is not oblivi-

ous to the difficult nature and necessities of planning and administration, it cannot conclude mere coincidence or that proper decision mechanisms resulted in the IEP's ultimate recommendation of 10 hours of in-school ABA services, the same "responsibility" listed by [the ABA supervisor] in contrast to [the private evaluator's] recommendation of 25-30 hours of home-based ABA.

While prior contemplation does not necessarily rise to the level of predetermination, the Court cannot ignore this evidence, which tends to show that the District did not come into the IEP meeting with an open mind, but rather predetermined at least one very significant component, namely the location and extent of ABA services that the District was willing to provide. This failure precluded genuine individualization of the child's IEP and deprived the Parents of a meaningful opportunity to participate in the development of the child's IEP.

Clearly, the cases reflect that as long as preparation and planning do not preclude full parental participation, preparatory activities are permissible. Permissible preparatory activities include the preparation of a draft IEP. However, when a draft IEP is prepared, the district must make clear through words and actions that the document is merely a draft or starting point.

The record of the IEP team meeting should reflect that the parents were afforded the opportunity to meaningfully participate in the development of their child's IEP. The following are some strategies for creating a record of meaningful participation:

✓ Provide a copy of the draft IEP to the parents in advance of the IEP team meeting, whenever possible;

✓ Document when parents are provided with copies of draft IEPs prior to the meeting;

✓ Write DRAFT at the top of each page, or across the page;

✓ Schedule the IEP team meeting to allow sufficient time for meaningful participation of all of the members including the parents;

✓ Record the time the meeting began and ended;

✓ Document changes made during the meeting;

✓ Document input from the parents that resulted in a specific change to the IEP; and

✓ Document parental participation in the meeting.

Full Participation of All IEP Team Members

The regulations set forth the members as follows:

The public agency must ensure that the IEP Team for each child with a disability includes —

(1) The parents of the child;

(2) Not less than one regular education teacher of the child (if the child is, or may be, participating in the regular education environment);

(3) Not less than one special education teacher of the child, or where appropriate, not less than one special education provider of the child;

(4) A representative of the public agency who —

(i) Is qualified to provide, or supervise the provision of, specially designed instruction to meet the unique needs of children with disabilities;

(ii) Is knowledgeable about the general education curriculum; and

(iii) Is knowledgeable about the availability of resources of the public agency.

(5) An individual who can interpret the instructional implications of evaluation results, who may be a member of the team described in paragraphs (a)(2) through (a)(6) of this section;

(6) At the discretion of the parent or the agency, other individuals who have knowledge or special expertise regarding the child, including related services personnel as appropriate; and

(7) Whenever appropriate, the child with a disability.

34 CFR 300.321(a).

The required IEP team must include a district representative. The district representative must be someone who, among other things, "is knowledgeable about the availability of resources of the public agency." 34 CFR 300.321(a)(4)(iii). The reason for this requirement is so that the district representative can commit the resources of the district during the meeting. In the *Mamaroneck Union Free School District* case discussed above, the district's ABA supervisor had written down a proposal but then did not attend the IEP meeting at which the proposal was presented. At the meeting, the team did not veer from the detailed proposal despite lengthy discussion, causing the court to conclude that they did not have an open mind. Perhaps the school district members of the IEP team felt they lacked the authority to offer something different from what the supervisor had written down prior to the meeting. That could explain why, according to the court, they did not genuinely consider any alternatives during the meeting. The person serving as the district representative in an IEP team meeting must have actual authority to commit resources. This role is a significant one, in that it allows the members to engage in a full discussion and genuinely entertain an array of options.

The regular education teacher of the child is another significant member of the IEP team. The hearing officer for the initial hearing that led to the case of *Deal ex rel. Deal v. Hamilton County Board of Education*, 42 IDELR 109, 392 F.3d 840 (6th Cir. 2004), *cert. denied*, 546 U.S. 936 (2005), noted multiple instances in which a regular education teacher had not been present at the student's IEP team meetings, calling these a "troubling procedural violation." The court explained the history as follows:

The ALJ found (1) that no regular education teacher attended the February 19, 1999, IEP meeting; (2) that no regular education teacher of Zachary's attended the October 15, 1998, IEP team meeting "even though it was clear that whether or not it would be appropriate for Zachary to participate in the regular education setting would be a subject of the meeting"; (3) that the regular education teacher who attended the August 25, 1999, meeting left before the 1999-2000 goals and objectives were developed and before the issue of placement was decided; and (4) that no regular education teacher attended the August 20, 1999, IEP meeting.

With respect to the August 1999 IEP team meetings, which were convened in order to develop an IEP for the child at a time when his parents were seeking greater integration for him in the regular classroom, the 6th U.S. Circuit Court of Appeals stated: "The absence of the unique perspective that could have been provided by a regular education teacher therefore had a real impact on the decision-making process." The court concluded further that this procedural violation constituted a denial of FAPE.[1]

The case of *M.L. v. Federal Way School District*, 105 LRP 13966, 394 F.3d 634 (9th Cir. 2005), *cert. denied*, 545 U.S. 1128 (2005), is an example of a case in which the absence of the regular education teacher was held to constitute a denial of FAPE. The case involved a child, M.L., who was born in 1994. He was identified as eligible for special education services as a student with autism and mental retardation (as well as macrocephaly), and was enrolled in a district's integrated preschool class with the same teacher, Jodie Wicks, from November 1997 through June 2000 (except for a few months during 1999-2000). Although some of his skills improved during that time, he simultaneously began to display "increasingly aggressive behavior" when frustrated or given challenging tasks.

M.L.'s IEP for 2000-2001 called for him to be enrolled in an integrated kindergarten class with "additional therapy and instructional services." However, before the year started, his family moved and he was enrolled in a different district (FWSD). His new school district initially implemented M.L.'s IEP from the previous district, which was set to expire on September 30, 2000, by enrolling him in an integrated kindergarten class taught by a teacher named Sandy Ramsey. During the first two weeks of September, however, his parents grew increasingly concerned about what they perceived to be teasing of M.L. by other students and insufficient responsiveness to the situation on the part of district personnel. M.L. stopped attending that particular school on September 11, 2000.

Approximately one week later, FWSD offered to enroll M.L. in a self-contained class in another school in the district. The parents disagreed because they wanted M.L. to continue to have opportunities to participate with regular education students. In October 2000, FWSD conducted a special education evaluation of M.L. in which no regular education teacher took part. The parents rejected FWSD's evaluation report and requested an independent evaluation, and FWSD filed a request for a due process hearing to establish the appropriateness of its evaluation.

FWSD also proposed to convene an IEP team meeting in November, and informed the parents that a regular education teacher would participate. However, due to a dispute over scheduling and location of the meeting, the parents did not attend. The meeting went forward as proposed on November 13 — without a regular education teacher in attendance, despite FWSD's previous assurance to the contrary.

Following this IEP team meeting, the district sent the resulting proposed IEP to the parents with an offer to meet to discuss and refine it, but the parents filed a request for a due process hearing instead. They claimed that FWSD's failure to include a regular education teacher on M.L.'s IEP team was a procedural violation that constituted a denial of FAPE.

The ALJ found that the IEP team "was appropriately constituted," and a district court subsequently upheld that ruling. On appeal, however, the 9th Circuit Court of Appeals vacated the district court's decision. First, after considering Congress's emphasis under IDEA 1997 on the importance of involvement in the regular curriculum for students with disabilities, the court concluded that "the failure to include at least one regular education teacher, standing alone, is a structural defect that prejudices the right of a disabled student to receive a FAPE." The 9th Circuit went on to reject the district's argument that because M.L. was unlikely to participate in an integrated classroom, a regular education teacher was not required to participate as a member of his IEP team. The court stated:

The FWSD argues that the participation of a regular education teacher on the IEP team was not required because it was not likely that M.L. would be placed in an integrated classroom since the Evaluation Report recommended against it. This argument completely ignores the fact that the record shows that the [the previous] IEP directed that M.L. be placed in a regular kindergarten classroom. M.L. had attended a regular preschool classroom for three years. After his family moved to the FWSD, M.L. was placed in Ms. Ramsey's regular education classroom. . . . In light of these facts, the record supports an inference that it was possible that M.L. would be placed in a regular education classroom. So long as this was a possibility, participation of a regular education teacher in the IEP team was required by the IDEA.

The FWSD was aware that two teachers had observed M.L. in an integrated classroom. Ms. Ramsey had observed him for one week before his mother withdrew him because he was teased by non-disabled children. Ms. Wicks had observed M.L. for three years in an integrated preschool classroom. Of the two regular education teachers, Ms. Wicks was the most knowledgeable about M.L.'s educational needs because she had been his teacher for three years. She recommended that M.L. be placed in an integrated classroom. The FWSD did not include either Ms. Ramsey or Ms. Wicks or any other regular education teacher on its IEP team.

The FWSD appears to suggest that the [parents] waived their right to object to the failure to include a regular education teacher on the IEP team because they failed to attend the IEP meetings. . . .

The FWSD's assumption-of-the-risk defense betrays its misunderstanding of the importance of the procedural requirements of the IDEA.

. . .

. . . Under the law of this circuit, the FWSD violated the procedural requirements of the IDEA, by failing to ensure the participation of a regular education teacher in the evaluation of M.L.'s educational needs.

In a concurring opinion, one 9th Circuit judge disagreed with the legal standard used by the majority in its analysis but agreed with the result:

The statutory requirement that an IEP team for a disabled child who is or may be in regular education must include a regular education teacher is not merely technical. A regular education teacher may have insights or perspectives that aid the process of IEP formation. We need not say that error in composition of an IEP team is always prejudicial and invariably results in the denial of a FAPE. Rather, we should assess the circumstances of each case, and here the record demonstrates that the failure to include Ms. Ramsey or Ms. Wicks or any other regular education teacher on the participating IEP team deprived M.L. of an educational opportunity.

The consequence of an improperly constituted IEP team in this case was significant. The 9th Circuit ruled: "This structural defect compels reversal of the district court's judgment without considering the merits of the IEP developed without the evaluation of at least one regular education teacher." The 9th Circuit reasoned that the merits of the IEP could not be considered because "the failure to include at least one regular education teacher, standing alone, is a structural defect that prejudices the right of a disabled student to receive a FAPE."

For the IEP team to be able to engage in genuine decision-making, it must be properly constituted. A duly constituted IEP team with full participation of all its members is what, according to the U.S. Supreme Court, helps ensure that the child receives a FAPE. The U.S. Supreme Court in *Board of Education v. Rowley* emphasized the importance of the process as follows:

> We think that the congressional emphasis upon full participation of concerned parties throughout the development of the IEP . . . demonstrates the legislative conviction that adequate compliance with the procedures prescribed would in most cases assure much if not all of what Congress wished in the way of substantive content in an IEP.[2]

Meaningful Parent Participation

As noted above, parents are required members of their child's IEP team under the federal IDEA regulations. School districts must be mindful of the premium that Congress and the U.S. Supreme Court have placed on parent participation in the IEP process. As the U.S. Supreme Court recently observed:

> The core of the statute . . . is the cooperative process that it establishes between parents and schools. *Rowley* [at 205-206] ("Congress placed every bit as much emphasis upon compliance with procedures giving parents and guardians a large measure of participation at every stage of the administrative process . . . as it did upon the measurement of the resulting IEP against a substantive standard.").[3]

Furthermore, case law has emphasized that parent "[p]articipation must be more than a mere form; it must be *meaningful*."[4] As is apparent from the cases in this book, in methodology disputes for children with autism spectrum disorders, a parent's claim that he or she was denied an opportunity for "meaningful participation" on an IEP team often goes hand in hand with a claim that the district predetermined the methodology and/or services for the child. That is, parents frequently make such claims when they perceive that they have been effectively shut out of the IEP team decision-making process.

Courts in autism spectrum disorder methodology disputes, therefore, typically review parents' claims of a denial of opportunity for "meaningful participation" in the IEP process in conjunction with the related issue of predetermination, and the courts' consideration of each case is necessarily fact-specific. The factors courts consider when evaluating such allegations include the following:

✓ Does the evidence (such as the child's IEP and testimony from IEP team members) demonstrate that the parents were afforded the opportunity to contribute input during IEP team meetings?

✓ Does the evidence (such as the child's IEP and testimony from IEP team members) demonstrate that the parents' requests, suggestions, concerns and other input were discussed and considered by the IEP team, even when such requests were contrary to district proposals?

✓ Does the evidence (such as the child's IEP and testimony from IEP team members) demonstrate that the IEP team incorporated at least some of the parents' requests and suggestions into operative sections of the child's IEP?

✓ Does the evidence (such as the child's IEP, a prior written notice and testimony from IEP team members) demonstrate that, if and when the parents' proposals were rejected, that district members of the IEP team explained the reasons for rejecting the parents' proposals?

The cases remind us that parents have perspectives and information about their children that no other IEP team member has. IDEA intends that parents, through their participation in the IEP process, will help shape their child's IEP. Despite a district's efforts to ensure meaningful participation, however, parents sometimes perceive that they have been shut out of the IEP process simply because the district does not agree to provide the services they request. Nevertheless, ensuring meaningful parent participation does not always mean doing what the parents want. Moreover, parents do not have line-item veto power over an IEP. Districts are ultimately responsible for ensuring that a FAPE is provided to each eligible child.

This chapter has emphasized the procedural requirement of a duly constituted IEP team, specifically, its membership and respective participatory roles. In struggling to find a substantive standard in the IDEA, the Supreme Court in *Rowley* (discussed in Chapter 1) ultimately concluded that, in most instances, if the procedures of the IDEA are followed, the right result will occur. The Supreme Court reasoned:

> When the elaborate and highly specific procedural safeguards embodied in [the IDEA] are contrasted with the general and somewhat imprecise substantive admonitions contained in the Act, we think that the importance Congress attached to these procedural safeguards cannot be gainsaid. . . . We think that the congressional emphasis upon full participation of concerned parties throughout the development of the IEP, as well as the requirements that state and local plans be submitted to the Secretary for approval, demonstrates the legislative conviction that adequate compliance with the procedures prescribed would in most cases assure much if not all of what Congress wished in the way of substantive content in an IEP.[5]

As discussed throughout this book, when school districts are on the losing end of a methodology dispute involving a child with an autism spectrum disorder, it is often not the result of the methodologies at issue, but other concerns. Therefore, districts should make methodology decisions in the context of overall sound educational programming for students with autism spectrum disorders, including compliance with the procedural requirements of the IDEA. The IEP must be developed by a team. The IEP team must be duly constituted. The IDEA specifies the team members because of the unique qualities that each of these members brings to the table. The professional members of the team contribute information that enables the parent to fully participate in the process. With a team that is both prepared and has an open mind, an individually tailored IEP can be developed. Chapter 8 provides specific guidance for developing an IEP for a child with an autism spectrum disorder.

ENDNOTES

[1] As with the 6th Circuit's 2004 conclusion in *Deal* that the school district had predetermined its methodology for Zachary, this procedural violation did not prove fatal in terms of the district's ability to utilize its chosen methodology with Zachary, because the subsequent remand to district court and a second appeal in 2008 to the 6th Circuit resulted in the conclusion that the district's program for him, including its chosen methodology, was appropriate. However, these findings of procedural violations did spur significant litigation, which was no doubt financially and emotionally costly for everyone involved.

[2] *Board of Educ. v. Rowley*, 553 IDELR 656 (EHLR 553:656), 458 U.S. 176, 206 (1982).

[3] *Schaffer v. Weast*, 44 IDELR 150, 526 U.S. 49, 53 (2005).

[4] *Deal ex rel. Deal v. Hamilton County Bd. of Educ.*, 42 IDELR 109, 392 F.3d 840, 858 (6th Cir. 2004), *cert. denied*, 546 U.S. 936 (2005) (emphasis in original) (citations omitted).

[5] *Board of Educ. v. Rowley*, 553 IDELR 656 (EHLR 553:656), 458 U.S. 176, 205-206 (1982).

Chapter 8

Developing an IEP

We know that the IEP must be "reasonably calculated to enable the child to receive educational benefits."[1] In order to assure that this substantive standard is satisfied, school district staff should enter the IEP process fully prepared with:

✓ a solid understanding of the nature of autism (Chapter 2);

✓ the appropriate training and expertise to plan and implement a comprehensive program for a child with an autism spectrum disorder, including an array of methodologies for use within a comprehensive program (Chapter 3);

✓ the ability to articulate a clear rationale for the methodologies they will use to implement the child's IEP (Chapter 3); and

✓ an understanding of what the research says regarding the methodologies for children with autism spectrum disorders (Chapter 4).

With the structure discussed in Chapters 2 through 4 in place, and with the benefit of a strong full and individual evaluation upon which to base an IEP (as discussed in Chapter 6), IEP teams should be well positioned to develop an individually tailored IEP.

This chapter addresses developing an individually tailored IEP for a child with an autism spectrum disorder, including the special factors that must be considered and addressed.

Does the IEP Have to Specify the Methodology?

It is clear from the cases that districts need to be prepared to have a discussion regarding methodology in the IEP team meeting. However, does the IEP have to specify the methodology?

Although the courts in some key cases have held that a district's failure to consider the methodology requested by the parents denied them meaningful participation in the IEP process, the USDE has long maintained that methodology does not have to be specified in the IEP unless doing so for a given child would be necessary for a FAPE.

As noted in Chapter 1, "special education" means:

> specially designed instruction, at no cost to the parents, to meet the unique needs of a child with a disability, including — (i) [i]nstruction conducted in the classroom, in the home, in hospitals and institutions, and in other settings; and (ii) [i]nstruction in physical education.

34 CFR 300.39(a)(1).

"Specially designed instruction" means:

> adapting, as appropriate to the needs of an eligible child under this part, the content, *methodology*, or delivery of instruction — (i) [t]o address the unique needs of the

child that result from the child's disability; and (ii) [t]o ensure access of the child to the general curriculum, so that the child can meet the educational standards within the jurisdiction of the public agency that apply to all children.

34 CFR 300.39(b)(3) (emphasis added).

The IEP must include:

A statement of the special education and related services and supplementary aids and services, based on peer-reviewed research to the extent practicable, to be provided to the child, or on behalf of the child, and a statement of the program modifications or supports for school personnel that will be provided. . . .

34 CFR 300.320(a)(4).

The position of the USDE regarding methodology was reaffirmed in its discussion of 34 CFR 300.320(a)(4):

We decline to require all IEP Team meetings to include a focused discussion on research-based methods or require public agencies to provide prior written notice when an IEP Team refuses to provide documentation of research-based methods, as we believe such requirements are unnecessary and would be overly burdensome.

. . .

There is nothing in the Act that requires an IEP to include specific instructional methodologies. Therefore, consistent with section 614(d)(1)(A)(ii)(I) of the Act,[2] we cannot interpret section 614 of the Act to require that all elements of a program provided to a child be included in an IEP. The Department's longstanding position on including instructional methodologies in a child's IEP is that it is an IEP Team's decision. Therefore, if an IEP Team determines that specific instructional methods are necessary for the child to receive FAPE, the instructional methods may be addressed in the IEP."

71 Fed. Reg. 46,665 (2006).

Therefore, the pivotal question regarding whether to specify a particular methodology in a child's IEP is whether or not it is necessary to do so to provide a FAPE. This point is underscored in the text of a guidance letter from the USDE's Office of Special Education Programs, in response to a parent's inquiry regarding whether or not school districts are required to provide phonics instruction to children with learning disabilities. The letter states:

[There is no] Federal law or regulation requiring States to use any specific instructional program for teaching children with learning disabilities. However, under Part B of the [IDEA], eligible children with one or more of thirteen specified disabilities, including children with specific learning disabilities, must receive special education and related services that they need to meet their individual needs.

. . .

If a child is determined to have a disability under Part B, the child's parents must have an opportunity to participate with school officials in designing his/her educational program. The vehicle for doing this is the IEP. Among other things, the IEP must contain a statement of the specific special education and related services to be provided to the child. Each child's educational program must be individually determined, and the child's placement must be based on his/her IEP. Part B provides for the active participation of parents in the development of their child's IEP. During the IEP meeting, it is appropriate for parents to bring their child's need[s] to the attention of school authorities. It would be appropriate to discuss the use of phonics to improve a child's reading skills during an IEP meeting.

Letter to Anonymous, 21 IDELR 573 (OSEP 1994).

(*See also Board of Educ. of New York City*, 5 ECLPR 71 (SEA NY 2007) ("Although an IEP must provide for specialized instruction in the child's areas of need, a[n IEP Team] is not required to specify methodology on an IEP. . . ."); *Letter to Hall*, 21 IDELR 58 (OSERS 1994) ("[W]hile Part B does mandate the required components to be included in each child's IEP to ensure that the child's identified educational needs can be addressed, Part B does not expressly mandate that the particular teacher, materials to be used, or instructional methods be included in a student's IEP."); *Central Bucks Sch. Dist.*, 40 IDELR 106 (SEA PA 2003) ("[T]he general rule is that methodology is not a required element of an IEP. . . ."); *Adams v. State of Oregon*, 31 IDELR 130, 195 F.3d 1141 (9th Cir. 1999) (The court upheld the appropriateness of the district's original IFSP, which reflected the IFSP team's purposeful decision "not to identify a specific methodology or program [for the child], so as not to be limited to only" DTT, the parents' preferred method.).)

As we have seen with the cases discussed throughout this book, courts expect IEP teams to be prepared to discuss the methodologies that may be appropriate for the child. If the parent asks the IEP team to consider a particular methodology, the team should engage in a genuine discussion about the issue, including discussion of the parent's preferred methodology. The discussion need not devolve, however, into a debate over which methods are better or best.

It may be sufficient to specify strategies and not the particular methodology in a child's IEP. The American Academy of Pediatrics published a 2007 clinical report that, without endorsing any particular methodology, states there is a "growing consensus" that an "effective early childhood intervention" for children with autism spectrum disorders includes "incorporation of a high degree of structure through elements such as predictable routine, visual activity schedules, and clear physical boundaries to minimize distractions."[3]

The full and individual evaluation should shed light on the range of methodologies that are appropriate to address the child's identified needs. Absent an indication that a methodology or methodologies must be specified in the IEP to ensure a FAPE, the methodology or methodologies should not have to be specified in the IEP. The IEP team should be prepared to specify the methodology in the IEP, however, if the child's unique needs make doing so necessary for FAPE (e.g., child's only form of communication is through PECS and the team agrees the child needs to continue to use PECS to communicate).

Furthermore, if the IEP team <u>does</u> specify a particular methodology in the IEP as necessary to provide a FAPE, then district personnel must be prepared to implement that methodology with fidelity. This point is illustrated by the case of *J.P. ex rel. Peterson v. County School Board of Hanover County, Va.*, 46 IDELR 133, 447 F. Supp. 2d 553 (E.D. Va. 2006), *judgment vacated by*, __ F.3d __ (4th Cir. 2008).

J.P. was a child with an autism spectrum disorder whose IEP required the provision of a "one-on-one teacher's aide who would be trained in the use of the discrete trial method," specifically in the processes of "repetition, data collection, [and] step by step methods, [which have been] proven to work with children with autism." Dissatisfied with the district's services for their child, J.P.'s parents filed a request for a due process hearing, alleging in pertinent part that that the district had failed to properly implement discrete trial methods. The hearing officer upheld the appropriateness of the school district's

IEPs for J.P., but on appeal a federal district court disagreed. Noting that the "discrete trial method is central to the ABA instructional method," the court concluded that the district's aide in this case (who had received only six days of training) had not been trained well enough to successfully implement discrete trial methods. The court's determination that the district had not implemented discrete trial methods with fidelity contributed to its conclusion that the district had failed to provide J.P. with an IEP that was reasonably calculated to provide a FAPE.

Although this decision was subsequently vacated by the 4th Circuit Court of Appeals in 2008, on the grounds that the district court had failed to give sufficient deference to the hearing officer's decision (*see J.P. ex rel. Peterson v. County Sch. Bd. of Hanover County, Va.*, __ F.3d __ (4th Cir. 2008)), the district court's ruling against the school district is still worth noting here because it demonstrates that courts do pay attention to whether districts are implementing their chosen methodologies with fidelity, particularly when the methodologies are specified in a child's IEP. Thus, when specifying a methodology in the IEP as necessary for FAPE, districts must have a thorough understanding of the implications of the methodology they agree to implement, and IEP teams should further consider, when necessary, related staff training needs as part of the IEP.

Addressing the Child's Individualized Needs Through an IEP

All of the specific components that must be addressed in a child's IEP arise from the requirement that the IEP be tailored to meet the child's unique needs. In *Dong v. Board of Education of Rochester Community School*, 31 IDELR 157, 197 F.3d 793 (6th Cir. 1999), the court stated:

> The decision not to provide the more intense one-on-one behavioral [DTT] therapy that the Dongs requested cannot be considered a failure to address Lisa's "unique needs." This was not a generic special education classroom that failed to meet the challenges of autistic impaired students or a situation where the child had some additional need outside the autistic impairment that was not addressed. Rather, the autistic impaired program recommended for Lisa was a 27.5 hour per week program with a staff to student ratio of one to two, and a mix of one-on-one and small group instruction, mainstreaming and reverse mainstreaming, in a functional language based program. Staff working with Lisa would include paraprofessionals, a teacher, a speech pathologist, and an occupational therapist. The school staff saw the TEACCH program as an opportunity for Lisa to learn generalization of language and spontaneous communication, independence, and social interaction; none of which would be stressed in a DTT program.

> Lisa's individual needs were addressed in designing the IEP in question.

(*See also Deal v. Hamilton County Dep't of Educ.*, 46 IDELR 45 (E.D. Tenn. 2006), *aff'd*, 49 IDELR 123 (6th Cir. 2008) (The court determined that the district's decision to provide an eclectic methodology for the child — instead of providing a program using ABA methodology as the parent requested — was appropriately tailored to meet the child's unique needs.).)

The IDEA specifies the information the IEP team must consider when developing an individually tailored IEP:

> In developing each child's IEP, the IEP team must consider —

> (i) The strengths of the child;

> (ii) The concerns of the parents for enhancing the education of their child;

(iii) The results of the initial or most recent evaluation of the child; and

(iv) The academic, developmental, and functional needs of the child.

34 CFR 300.324(a)(1).

Special Factors

In addition to the above considerations, there also are certain special factors that the IEP team must consider when developing a child's IEP. These factors include behavior strategies when the child's behavior interferes with learning (*see* 34 CFR 300.324(a)(2)(i)); the language needs of a limited English proficient child with disabilities (*see* 34 CFR 300.324(a)(2)(ii)); the use of Braille for a child who is blind or visually impaired (*see* 34 CFR 300.324(a)(2)(iii)); the communication needs of the child (*see* 34 CFR 300.324(a)(2)(iv)); and whether the child needs assistive technology devices and services (*see* 34 CFR 300.324(a)(2)(v)). These special factors shape the content of the IEP.

The special factors that are most often the subject of litigation involving children with autism spectrum disorders are behavior, communication, and assistive technology. As the cases illustrate, the failure to adequately consider these special factors and address them, as needed, in the child's IEP can make the school district vulnerable in a methodology dispute.

IEP Team Must Consider Use of Positive Behavioral Interventions, Supports, and Other Strategies to Address Certain Behaviors

In developing the IEP, the IEP team must:

> In the case of a child whose behavior impedes the child's learning or that of others, consider the use of positive behavioral interventions and supports, and other strategies, to address that behavior. . . .

34 CFR 300.324(a)(2)(i).

The 2007 clinical report from the American Academy of Pediatrics states that there is a "growing consensus" that an "effective early childhood intervention" for children with autism spectrum disorders includes "use of assessment-based curricula that address . . . reduction of disruptive or maladaptive behavior by using empirically supported strategies, including functional assessment."[4]

The case of *County School Board of Henrico County, VA v. R.T.*, 45 IDELR 274, 433 F. Supp. 2d 657 (E.D. Va. 2006), illustrates how some of the behavioral characteristics of children with autism spectrum disorders can significantly interfere with all facets of the child's learning. As discussed extensively in earlier chapters, this case involved a young boy whose parents, concerned about his lack of progress in the district's preschool program, implemented an intensive at-home program of ABA methodology for the child and thereafter requested that the district provide this program at public expense. The district did not do so, and instead proposed an IEP that essentially replicated the methodology and services that had failed to enable RT to make progress in the past. The parents withdrew RT from the district, enrolled him in private school (Faison), and challenged the district's IEP in a due process hearing and in federal court, where they prevailed. The court's decision provides an explanation of some of the behavioral characteristics of autism spectrum disorders that significantly impact learning:

> Related to the fact that autistic people are often in their own worlds and do not pay attention to normal stimuli, autistic people will frequently engage in self-stimulating

behaviors called "stimming" in the jargon of the study of autism. Among autistic children, stimming may be displayed, for example, in the form of rocking back and forth, flapping one's hands repetitively, groaning or murmuring, or, in the case of young children, mouthing objects such as toys as a means of stimulus rather than engaging in normal play activities. When an autistic child is engaged in stimming behaviors, it [*sic*] is not able to focus on other stimuli such as educational instruction.

The district court's ruling in the parents' favor was based in large part on its determination that the school district had ignored evidence from Mr. and Mrs. T. regarding their success using ABA to address RT's behavioral issues, and had instead persisted in implementing the TEACCH methodology despite evidence that it was not helping RT to make progress. The court made the following findings:

- While enrolled in the [district's preschool] program, "RT engaged in self-stimming, would flap his hands especially when he was excited, and . . . had a difficult time focusing[ ]";

- During summer of 2002, "RT lacked attending skills, was highly distracted, and engaged in self-stimulatory behaviors," which made it very difficult to get and keep his attention;

- Once his at-home ABA providers during summer 2002 "were able to get RT's stimming under control, he was better able to attend to task," leading to "consistent learning";

- Mrs. T. shared information about RT's progress using ABA with Twin Hickory's IEP team;

- An evaluation performed by a district speech pathologist in October 2002 indicated that RT had improved his social integration skills while in the PEDD program but not his verbalization skills, and that he engaged in self-stimming; and

- The doctor in charge of Faison evaluated RT in July 2002 and found that he "engaged in a high frequency of self-stimulating activities, 'was basically not able to engage in any purposeful activity,' and was non-verbal."

Based on this and other evidence, the court ultimately held that Twin Hickory's November 2002 IEP "was not reasonably calculated to provide RT with the requisite benefit":

> The evidence demonstrated clearly that in the fall of 2002 RT engaged in a high frequency of self-stimulatory behaviors that interfered with his ability to learn, lacked all but the most basic attending skills, did not possess joint attention or imitation skills. Absent these skills, and until the stimming was brought under control, RT could not make any more than de minimis educational progress. The preponderance of the evidence also demonstrated that for RT to learn these skills and to stop stimming, RT required a rigorous, intensive education program of between 20 and 40 hours of instruction per week. The fifteen hours of instruction provided by the November IEP was insufficient. Moreover, the preponderance of the evidence demonstrated that to learn attending skills, reduce the stimming, and learn imitation skills, RT required a highly structured, highly focused education methodology such as ABA therapy in which RT would receive intensive one-on-one instruction.

The IDEA and its implementing regulations do not specifically require a functional behavioral assessment or a behavior intervention plan outside of the disciplinary change of placement context:

Under 34 CFR 300.324(a)(2)(i), the use of positive behavioral interventions and supports must be considered in the case of a child whose behavior impedes his or her learning or that of others. The requirement that a child with a disability receive, as appropriate, a functional behavioral assessment and a behavioral intervention plan and modifications designed to address the child's behavior now only applies to students whose behavior is a manifestation of their disability as determined by the LEA, the parent, and the relevant members of the child's IEP Team under 34 CFR 300.530(e).[5]

However, a functional behavioral assessment should be conducted and a behavior intervention plan developed *as needed* to address the individualized needs of the child:

Under 34 CFR 300.324(a)(2), in developing an IEP for a student whose behavior impedes his or her learning or that of others, the IEP Team must consider the use of positive behavioral interventions and supports, and other strategies, to address the behavior. As part of this determination, an IEP Team may decide that an FBA and BIP are appropriate interventions and supports. Nothing in these regulations prohibits an IEP Team from determining, in other situations, that an FBA or BIP is appropriate for a child.[6]

In *Escambia County Board of Education v. Benton*, 44 IDELR 272, 406 F. Supp. 2d 1248 (S.D. Ala. 2005), the parent claimed that the school district violated the IDEA by failing to address her son's behavioral needs in the IEP. Despite having requested that Benton's behavior be addressed as part of his IEP over the course of developing 11 IEPs with the district, no behavior component was ever included. At the due process hearing, the school district's autism expert testified

that Benton did not require a functional behavior analysis or behavior intervention plan because his behaviors were characteristic of autism, that he had observed no aggressive behavior from Benton during a three-hour observation session, that any inappropriate behaviors by Benton were successfully managed by school personnel, and that the school system appeared to be managing Benton appropriately via one-on-one instruction in a predictable, structured environment. The expert attributed Benton's disruptive conduct at the hearing to the effects of being in a strange room with strange people, outside of a structured classroom environment, and opined that Benton had displayed no signs of aggression.

The hearing officer, however, concluded "that Benton's right to a FAPE was compromised by the [district's] failure 'to conduct a functional behavior assessment and to draft and implement either an appropriate behavior intervention plan or to revise [Benton's] IEPs to address [his] autistic behavior.'" In the subsequent appeal to federal district court, the court, like the hearing officer, was not persuaded by the school district's argument "that because Benton's classroom behaviors are a natural outgrowth or byproduct of his autism, no behavioral plan was needed." The court explained:

To the extent that the [district] does adopt that tack, the undersigned concurs with the Hearing Officer that "[t]he fact that the behaviors demonstrated by the child are a manifestation of [his] autism does not excuse a school system from providing behavior management techniques either in the child's IEP or in a separately formulated behavior intervention plan." . . . "[G]ood professional practice dictates that you determine interventions based on the unique needs of each child," rather than categorically stating (as the IEPs did) that no behavioral intervention is needed because the behaviors in question arise from autism. . . . Thus, extensive evidence at the due process hearing refutes the school system's convoluted and demonstratively flawed rationale that no behavior plan was warranted because the behaviors at issue related to Benton's disability.

In the case of *Neosho R-V School District v. Clark*, 38 IDELR 61, 315 F.3d 1022 (8th Cir. 2003), the 8th Circuit Court of Appeals upheld a district court's determination that the school district's failure to provide an appropriate behavior intervention plan for a child with an autism spectrum disorder constituted a denial of a FAPE. Robert, who was 12 years old during the 1997-1998 school year, was prone to problem behaviors as a result of his Asperger's Disorder, "which, when unmanaged, largely prevent[ed] him from interacting with his peers in an acceptable manner." Prior to the beginning of that school year, his parents had filed a request for a due process hearing against the district, resulting in a settlement agreement which, in pertinent part, "required the School District to provide specific interventions and strategies to manage Robert's inappropriate behavior." Despite this, the district's August 1997 and October 1997 IEPs for Robert "stated that a behavior plan was attached to them, but the attachments were merely short-term goals and objectives that did not provide specific interventions and strategies to manage Robert's behavior problems."

Robert's special education teacher and the paraprofessional required by his IEP tried their best to manage his behavior using various strategies, none of which had "been actually analyzed or approved by Robert's IEP team." Moreover, although the IEP team had "agreed that a new behavior management plan was necessary to meet Robert's needs during the 1997-98 school year . . . [and] that the new plan should not be based on Robert's past behavior," a new plan was not timely developed. Instead, Robert's special education teacher and paraprofessional used a checklist from an outside agency's plan from the previous school year which had never been adopted by his IEP team. In addition, his teacher "did not begin to formally chart data in a format that could be used to develop a new behavior management plan until March 1998."

Despite a dramatic increase in Robert's problem behaviors during that year — behaviors that "prevented him from being included in mainstreamed classes beyond music and substantially interfered with his ability to learn" — the district did not try to develop a new plan to address his behavior until the school year was almost over.

Robert's parents filed a request for a due process hearing to challenge the district's failure to develop a cohesive, timely behavior intervention plan as required by his IEP, and the hearing officer ruled in the parents' favor. In the school district's subsequent appeal to federal district court, the parents again prevailed on that issue. The school district then appealed the case to the 8th Circuit Court of Appeals, contending that Robert's IEPs had in fact appropriately addressed his behavior issues and had provided him with a FAPE. In support, the district pointed to report cards and other evidence in the record which, it asserted, demonstrated that Robert had made progress under the 1997-1998 IEPs. However, the 8th Circuit also ruled in the parents' favor on this issue, stating:

> Our independent review convinces us that because the IEPs did not appropriately address his behavior problem, Robert was denied a free appropriate public education.

> The [parents'] expert witness testified that the papers attached to the IEPs were not sufficient to amount to a cohesive behavior management plan. Witnesses confirmed that such a plan was never adopted by the IEP team, in spite of the fact that Robert's behavior problem was the major concern at every IEP meeting. . . . The fact that no cohesive [behavior intervention] plan was in place to meet Robert's behavioral needs supports the ultimate conclusion that he was not able to obtain a benefit from his education.

In contrast, in the case of *W.S. ex rel. C.S. v. Rye City Sch. Dist.*, 46 IDELR 285, 454 F. Supp. 2d 134 (S.D.N.Y. 2006), the court concluded that the district's functional behavioral assessment (FBA) was both timely (in that it was conducted prior to the finalization of the final July 2005 IEP, in response to concerns about the child's persistent "stereotypical autistic behaviors" and regression documented in May 2005) and proper (in that it contained all elements required by state law). "It set forth the reason for the referral, identified the problem behaviors and their triggers, concurrences and consequences," the *W.S.* court said. "It indicated what negative reinforcements cause [the child] to maintain the behaviors. It set behavioral goals, listed eight strategies for helping [her] achieve those goals, and devised 'prompts' to use when advising her about what was expected of her. . . . Teachers found that [the child] could be refocused or redirected when she began engaging in inappropriate behaviors."

When the function of a behavior is properly explored and understood by the IEP team, the team can identify the appropriate strategies to address the behavior. In *CM by JM and EM v. Board of Public Education of Henderson County*, 36 IDELR 96, 184 F. Supp. 2d 466 (W.D.N.C. 2002), the school district believed that tantrumming by a child with an autism spectrum disorder served to function as a means of communication:

> McDanel testified that tantrumming is the beginning level of communication for autistic children and as soon as they have a system to communicate, the tantrums decrease. They are allowed to use pictures or other methods to communicate their needs and then the behavior usually ceases. "I rarely have anybody tantrumming, because academically they're learning." Tantrums are a sign, not that the child is lazy, but that he or she is sick, hungry, tired, or frustrated.

Although the parent in this case preferred the Lovaas methodology, the court deferred to the district's determination to offer the TEACCH methodology to CM. As this case illustrates, when the individual needs, including the behavioral needs, of a child with an autism spectrum disorder are adequately analyzed and addressed as part of the IEP process, courts will likely show greater deference to the district's methodology choices. As the CM court concluded, "Indeed, it may well be that the TEACCH program would have provided a superior model for CM's emotional and social development."

IEP Team Must Consider Communication Needs of the Child

In developing the IEP, the IEP team must "[c]onsider the communication needs of the child." 34 CFR 300.324(a)(2)(iv). Children with autism spectrum disorders may demonstrate a wide range of needs for special education and related services in the area of communication. Indeed, communication issues may be among the first problems noted by parents, prompting them to seek evaluations.

When developing the IEP, the team must carefully consider and address these needs in the child's IEP. Many children with autism spectrum disorders require fundamental support in functional communication skill development in addition to other types of speech therapy services, for the following reason:

> [W]hat distinguishes children with autism from other language handicapped people is not so much the words, although a lot of kids have great difficulty learning words, it's using those words in a social context to communicate naturally, spontaneously, and meaningfully.[7]

The previously cited 2007 clinical report from the American Academy of Pediatrics states that there is a "growing consensus" that an "effective early childhood intervention" for children with autism spectrum disorders includes "use of assessment-based curricula that address . . . functional, spontaneous communication."[8]

A case discussed extensively in earlier chapters of this book is an example of IEP team decision-making and communication-related service provision that withstood a legal challenge and was deemed appropriate by a reviewing court. As noted previously, the school district in *J.P. ex rel. Popson v. West Clark Community Schools*, 38 IDELR 5, 230 F. Supp. 2d 910 (S.D. Ind. 2002), determined through its evaluation process that 3-year-old J.P. had several specific skill deficits, including many in the area of communication. Based on its evaluation, the district recommended a program of special education and related services that offered the child "an opportunity to learn a functional communication system" and "speech therapy to address his functional communication difficulties."

After implementing its initial IEP (which called for (among other things) 80 minutes per week of speech therapy) for approximately three months, the IEP team reviewed J.P.'s progress and determined that although he had made progress in a variety of areas, his functional communication skills remained weak. Based on this information, the committee developed new communication goals for J.P. and also "determined that [he] should receive extended school year (ESY) services focusing upon his communication skills in order to avoid substantial regression of those skills during the summer." The parents challenged the sufficiency of the amount of speech therapy ESY in the legal dispute, but the court ruled in favor of the school district.

As noted earlier in this book, the parents also challenged the district's use of an eclectic instructional approach rather than exclusively using the ABA methodology they preferred. The court ruled in favor of the district's methodology choices, noting many features that demonstrated that the IEP was specifically tailored to J.P.'s unique needs and therefore reasonably calculated to provide him with a FAPE. Among the factors deemed persuasive by the court was the testimony of J.P.'s speech therapist, who stated that,

> by using ABA/DTT methods, J.P. had made substantial progress in learning to vocalize. But she pointed out that he still was not communicating because he had not yet grasped the communicative intent of the sounds he was making. Her testimony made clear that she understood the difference between "vocalizing" and "communicating," and believed that the overarching goal of achieving functional communication *would be best facilitated by means other than just discrete trial training*. (Emphasis added.)

Thus, the record established that the district's decision to implement an eclectic approach for J.P. rather than an exclusive program of ABA/DTT methodology was based on a considered, individualized determination as to how best to meet the child's unique needs, including his communication needs. The district prevailed in the court case as a result. (*See also Dong v. Board of Educ. of Rochester Community Schs.*, 31 IDELR 157, 197 F.3d 793 (6th Cir. 1999) (The court approved of the district's decision to use the TEACCH methodology rather than the intensive, 40-hour per week, one-on-one DTT program the parents sought. The court concluded that the district's IEP was appropriately tailored to meet Lisa's individual needs, noting in particular that "[t]he school staff saw the TEACCH program as an opportunity for Lisa to learn generalization of *language and spontaneous communication*, independence, and social interaction; none of which would be stressed in a DTT program.") (Emphasis added.).)

IEP Team Must Consider Whether the Child Needs Assistive Technology Devices and Services

In developing the IEP, the IEP team must "[c]onsider whether the child needs assistive technology devices and services." 34 CFR 300.324(a)(2)(v).

"Assistive technology device" is defined as meaning:

[A]ny item, piece of equipment, or product system, whether acquired commercially off the shelf, modified, or customized, that is used to increase, maintain, or improve the functional capabilities of a child with a disability. The term does not include a medical device that is surgically implanted, or the replacement of such device. 34 CFR 300.5.

"Assistive technology service" is defined as meaning:

[A]ny service that directly assists a child with a disability in the selection, acquisition, or use of an assistive technology device. The term includes —

(a) The evaluation of the needs of a child with a disability, including a functional evaluation of the child in the child's customary environment;

(b) Purchasing, leasing, or otherwise providing for the acquisition of assistive technology devices by children with disabilities;

(c) Selecting, designing, fitting, customizing, adapting, applying, maintaining, repairing, or replacing assistive technology devices;

(d) Coordinating and using other therapies, interventions, or services with assistive technology devices, such as those associated with existing education and rehabilitation plans and programs;

(e) Training or technical assistance for a child with a disability or, if appropriate, that child's family; and

(f) Training or technical assistance for professionals (including individuals providing education or rehabilitation services), employers, or other individuals who provide services to, employ, or are otherwise substantially involved in the major life functions of that child.

34 CFR 300.6.

For children with autism spectrum disorders, it is often their communication needs that give rise to the need for assistive technology devices and services, in the form of either low tech (i.e., without reliance on electricity) or high tech (e.g., voice-output devices) assistive technology. PECS is one instructional methodology that uses assistive technology devices to improve the functional capabilities of children with autism spectrum disorders in the area of symbolic communication. Instructional personnel who use PECS generally employ low-tech devices, such as printed pictures or symbols, communication strips, and notebooks, to teach children how to use symbolic communication. The pictures generally are printed at school and laminated for durability. Velcro is attached to the backside of each picture so a child may affix it to a communication strip or store it in a personal communication notebook. A child first learns to request desired items or activities by removing a picture from the notebook and delivering it to an adult in exchange for the item or activity. Repeated practice of such exchanges teaches the child that pictures are symbols representing desired items or activities. Later, a child learns to affix multiple pictures to a communication strip in order to form sentences. In advanced stages of PECS, each child carries a personal communication notebook to facilitate communication throughout the day.

In a case involving a program administered under the IDEA Part C (for children from birth through age 2), the district court in *Andrew M. and Dierdre M. v. Delaware County Office of Mental Health and Mental Retardation*, 44 IDELR 92 (E.D. Pa. 2005), concluded that the county early intervention providers denied FAPE to a young boy with an autism spectrum disorder by failing to develop an IFSP for him that appropriately addressed his severe functional communication skill deficits.

Although the regulatory requirements governing the development and content of a child's IFSP are not exactly the same as those governing IEP development and content, there are substantial similarities, including that the IFSP must contain specific information regarding the child's present levels, needs and services pertaining to communication skills. (*See* 34 CFR 303.12, 303.344.) Under IDEA Part B, for a child ages 3 through 5:

> The IFSP may serve as the IEP of the child, if using the IFSP as the IEP is —
>
> (i) Consistent with State policy; and
>
> (ii) Agreed to by the agency and the child's parents.

34 CFR 300.323(b)(1).

As described in *Andrew M.*, P.M. and his twin brother R.M. were both found to have "significant speech and language delays" by the time they were one year old, "and P.M. was eventually diagnosed with" a pervasive developmental disorder. Furthermore,

> [e]ach boy had behavioral issues arising out of frustration at his inability to communicate. R.M. would cry a lot. P.M. would become physically aggressive when he was frustrated, and would scratch the face and neck of whoever was with him, whether it was an adult or another child.

In Delaware County, Pa., where the boys lived, the state's IDEA Part C "Early Intervention Program for [eligible] children from birth to age three [was] administered by the county Office of Mental Health and Mental Retardation [MH/MR]." IFSPs were developed for both boys that provided for speech therapy services. The court notes that P.M. was also "found eligible to receive mental health 'wraparound' services . . . and received assistance from [a] therapeutic support staff aide ('TSS')."

Around this time, the boys' mother learned about the benefits of the PECS system for developing children's functional communication skills. (The court's decision describes PECS instruction as taking place in specific phases, noting in relevant part that "it is the recognition of PECS as a mode of communication, as acquired in Phase Two, which makes PECS a true communication system.") More specifically, she learned about gains achieved by children who had attended a two-week PECS summer camp program coupled with follow-up in-home PECS consultant services. She contacted the twins' early intervention service coordinator and asked if the boys could attend the camp and obtain follow-up consultation at public expense. The coordinator said that he would check with his supervisor.

Meanwhile, however, the mother contacted the PECS camp directly and learned that camp for the summer already had occurred that year, so she arranged for in-home consultation services from a provider with the PECS camp without the involvement of MH/MR. The parents' goal was to obtain training for themselves and their au pair as to how to implement PECS with the twins in their home.

Unfortunately, although the boys showed progress when the consultant implemented PECS activities with them directly, this success did not carry over to other times:

> Despite [the consultant's] positive notes, [the mother] testified, the boys were not accepting PECS as a form of communication, and were becoming deeply frustrated every day. . . .
>
> . . .
>
> [The mother testified that P.M.] is so frustrated that he's not getting what he wants. . . . The more we put the PECS book in front of him, the more he just, you know, just gets madder and then he just — you know, something explodes in him and he physically goes for you, and then we see him that he zones out after. Obviously, he puts a lot into this because, you know, I have scars around my neck. . . .

Still believing that more intensive PECS instruction and support was necessary, especially for P.M., the twins' parents again requested that MH/MR allow the boys to attend PECS camp the next summer. A MH/MR supervisor declined the request, so the parents requested an administrative review meeting with MH/MR personnel. Two meetings were held, during which time various non-treating MH/MR administrators met with the boys' providers and reviewed their IFSPs and progress documentation. The MH/MR administrators then reiterated the agency's refusal to fund the PECS camp, asserting both that the camp was an unjustifiable departure from the "natural environment" requirement for IFSPs and that the boys were making progress without the camp.

The parents filed a request for a due process hearing to challenge this decision, but the hearing officer concluded that the IFSPs for both boys were appropriate, based in large part on a finding that "the children have experienced growth and progress with the existing IFSPs." Before this decision was issued, the parents enrolled both of their sons in the PECS camp on their own. When they received notice of the hearing officer's decision and realized that they would not be reimbursed for the camp tuition, they withdrew R.M. but paid the $3,000 fee for P.M. to attend, as his "communication needs were more severe." According to the mother's later testimony during the subsequent appeal of the case to federal court, "PECS camp was wonderful for P.M.," in that it enabled him to communicate for the first time and lessened his frustration.

At the court hearing, the parents' expert (a speech pathologist) testified that PECS camp was necessary for P.M. to learn critical functional communication skills:

> [F]or the previous 7 months, despite the training he was receiving, he was making very, very minimal progress and there [were] parent frustrations, behavioral outbursts, and the family was not able to communicate with him, he was not communicating with the family. He wasn't growing. He wasn't learning. And it *became apparent that he required the structure and intensity of a more dense program, such as what they offered at the camp so he could be saturated with the exchange system.*

> . . . [After PECS camp, P.M.] was a communicator. He had learned the routine of using pictures — picture exchange to communicate requests and to discriminate between objects, and was starting to use sentence strips, and actually had started to vocalize and to verbalize along with his use of the pictures. By report, there was a significant change in his use of communication and his behavior. (Emphasis added.)

The district court ruled in favor of the parents, concluding that the failure to provide the PECS camp for P.M. had rendered his IFSP "defective."[9] The court determined that MH/MR had sufficient information at the time of the parents' request for the PECS camp to realize that the provision of this camp for P.M. should have been, "at the least, a matter for further inquiry."

> [T]he decisionmakers . . . had available to them information from both [parents], the children's speech therapist, their classroom teacher, and P.M.'s TSS, that *the skills [the consultant] was developing in controlled circumstances were not carrying over into the boys' everyday lives.* All parties concerned agreed that this was particularly problematic for P.M., because he was not acquiring spoken language, and because he became violently upset when frustrated. (Emphasis added.)

Accordingly, the court held that "P.M.'s IFSP was inadequate without the inclusion of the PECS camp . . . [because] the intensive experience offered by the camp was necessary to permit P.M. to make meaningful progress toward his IFSP goals."

While the methodology does not have to be specified as part of the IEP unless necessary for a FAPE, the IEP must be individualized. There are certain special factors that must be considered when developing a child's IEP. The special factors shape the content of the IEP. Consideration of the special factors, particularly behavior, communication and the assistive technology needs of a child with an autism spectrum disorder, leads to a highly individualized IEP. Chapter 9 guides school districts through the content requirements of the IEP.

ENDNOTES

[1] *Board of Educ. v. Rowley*, 553 IDELR 656 (EHLR 553:656), 458 U.S. 176, 207 (1982).

[2] 20 USC 1414(d)(1)(A)(ii)(I) of the IDEA 2004 states that nothing in that section of the Act (describing the required elements of an IEP) "shall be construed to require . . . that additional information be included in a child's IEP beyond what is explicitly required in this section. . . ."

[3] Myers, Scott M., M.D. (2007). Management of children with autism spectrum disorders. *Pediatrics,* vol. 120: num. 5:1163.

[4] Myers, Scott M., M.D. (2007). Management of children with autism spectrum disorders. *Pediatrics,* vol. 120: num. 5:1163-1164.

[5] *OSERS Questions and Answers on Discipline Procedures, Q/A #E-1*, 47 IDELR 227 (OSERS 2007).

[6] *OSERS Questions and Answers on Discipline Procedures, Q/A #E-2*, 47 IDELR 227 (OSERS 2007).

[7] *CM by JM and EM v. Board of Pub. Educ. of Henderson County*, 36 IDELR 96, 184 F. Supp. 2d 466, 475 (W.D.N.C. 2002) (citation omitted).

[8] Myers, Scott M., M.D. (2007). Management of children with autism spectrum disorders. *Pediatrics,* vol. 120: num. 5:1163.

[9] The court determined that R.M.'s IFSP was not similarly flawed, because R.M. had been making more progress than P.M., even without the PECS camp.

Chapter 9

Content of the IEP

When Congress reauthorized the IDEA in 2004, it directed the U.S. Secretary of Education to develop model forms including a model IEP as follows:

> Not later than the date that the Secretary publishes final regulations under this chapter, to implement amendments made by the Individuals with Disabilities Education Improvement Act of 2004, the Secretary shall publish and disseminate widely to States, local educational agencies, and parent and community training and information centers . . . a model IEP form. . . .

20 USC 1417(e).

The model form that was developed and published by the U.S. Secretary of Education in 2006 largely tracks the regulations, although in some cases it uses language that the Secretary considers "more user-friendly" than that found in the regulations. Taken directly from the model form, the IEP must contain:

A statement of the child's present levels of academic achievement and functional performance including:

- How the child's disability affects the child's involvement and progress in the general education curriculum (i.e., the same curriculum as for nondisabled children) or for preschool children, as appropriate, how the disability affects the child's participation in appropriate activities. (*See* 34 CFR 300.320(a)(1).)

A statement of measurable annual goals, including academic and functional goals designed to:

- Meet the child's needs that result from the child's disability to enable the child to be involved in and make progress in the general education curriculum. (*See* 34 CFR 300.320(a)(2)(i)(A).)

- Meet each of the child's other educational needs that result from the child's disability. (*See* 34 CFR 300.320(a)(2)(i)(B).)

- For children with disabilities who take alternate assessments aligned to alternate achievement standards, a description of benchmarks or short-term objectives (in addition to the annual goals). (*See* 34 CFR 300.320(a)(2)(ii).)

A description of:

- How the child's progress toward meeting the annual goals will be measured. (*See* 34 CFR 300.320(a)(3)(i).)

When periodic reports on the progress the child is making toward meeting the annual goals will be provided, such as through the use of quarterly or other periodic reports, concurrent with the issuance of report cards. (*See* 34 CFR 300.320(a)(3)(ii).)

A statement of the special education and related services and supplementary aids and services, based on peer-reviewed research to the extent practicable, to be provided to the child, or on behalf of the child, and a statement of the program modifications or supports for school personnel that will be provided to enable the child:

- To advance appropriately toward attaining the annual goals. (*See* 34 CFR 300.320(a)(4)(i).)

- To be involved in and make progress in the general education curriculum and to participate in extracurricular and other nonacademic activities. (*See* 34 CFR 300.320(a)(4)(ii).)

- To be educated and participate with other children with disabilities and nondisabled children in extracurricular and other nonacademic activities. (*See* 34 CFR 300.320(a)(4)(iii).)

An explanation of the extent, if any, to which the child will not participate with nondisabled children in the regular classroom and in extracurricular and other nonacademic activities. (*See* 34 CFR 300.320(a)(5).)

A statement of any individual appropriate accommodations that are necessary to measure the academic achievement and functional performance of the child on state and districtwide assessments. (*See* 34 CFR 300.320(a)(6)(i).)

If the IEP team determines that the child must take an alternate assessment instead of a particular regular state or districtwide assessment of student achievement, a statement of why:

- The child cannot participate in the regular assessment. (*See* 34 CFR 300.320(a)(6)(ii)(A).)

- The particular alternate assessment selected is appropriate for the child. (*See* 34 CFR 300.320(a)(6)(ii)(B).)

The projected date for the beginning of special education and related services and supplementary aids and services and modifications and supports, and the anticipated frequency, location, and duration of the services and modifications. (*See* 34 CFR 300.320(a)(7).)

Beginning not later than the first IEP to be in effect when the child turns 16, or younger if determined appropriate by the IEP team, and updated annually thereafter, the IEP must include:

- Appropriate measurable postsecondary goals based upon age-appropriate transition assessments related to training, education, employment, and, where appropriate, independent living skills. (*See* 34 CFR 300.320(b)(1).)

- The transition services (including courses of study) needed to assist the child in reaching those goals. (*See* 34 CFR 300.320(b)(2).)

(U.S. Department of Education Model Form: IEP, located at: *http://idea.ed.gov/static /modelForms.*)

While all of these are essential components of the IEP for any child with a disability, including an IDEA-eligible child who has an autism spectrum disorder, the focus of this chapter is on those elements that most often have been the subject of litigation.

Statement of the Child's Present Levels of Academic Achievement and Functional Performance

The IEP must contain a statement of the child's "present levels of academic achievement and functional performance." 34 CFR 300.320(a)(1). The child's present levels of academic achievement and functional performance are what drive the annual goals. The child's present levels also establish the baseline by which subsequent progress can be gauged.

In the case of *Kirby v. Cabell County Board of Education*, 46 IDELR 156 (S.D. W. Va. 2006), Robert Kirby was 18 years old at the time the district court's decision was issued. He had been receiving special education services from the school district since fourth grade as a child with multiple disabilities, including Asperger's Disorder. When he was 16, before he began 11th grade, a dispute arose between his parents and the school district that resulted in the parents filing a request for a due process hearing on claims that (among other things) the district had "failed to provide appropriate comprehensive evaluations of Robert and failed to follow the recommendations provided by the independent evaluators obtained by the parents." The parents also alleged that that the district's proposed IEP for the upcoming 2004-2005 school year was not reasonably calculated to provide a FAPE.

The hearing officer ruled in the school district's favor, despite finding that the district's documentation of Robert's present levels of academic achievement and functional performance was flawed. However, a district court, on appeal, criticized the hearing officer's reasoning and conclusion:

> The IHO concluded that the IEP was sufficient but directed additional testing to document the student's level of academic achievement through objective, standardized tests. In her brief discussion of this point, the IHO noted that Robert's past achievement tests showed some gains but also declines in his academic progress. She rejected the claim that Robert's teachers had inflated his grades just to pass him, but she found that standardized, objective tests were necessary to measure his specific subject area mastery. Despite this deficiency in the IEP, the IHO upheld the IEP. The Court finds this reasoning flawed. If the IEP fails to assess the "child's present levels of academic achievement and functional performance," the IEP does not comply with [the IDEA]. This deficiency goes to the heart of the IEP; the child's level of academic achievement and functional performance is the foundation on which the IEP must be built. Without a clear identification of Robert's present levels, the IEP cannot set measurable goals, evaluate the child's progress, and determine which educational and related services are needed.

Because of this insufficiency of the present levels of academic achievement and functional performance, the district court concluded that Robert's IEP failed to provide him with a FAPE, and it ordered the parties "to reconvene an IEP meeting with a facilitator to develop an IEP which consider[ed] Robert's current levels of achievement and functional performance with a specific plan to address his deficiencies."

(*See also Escambia County Bd. of Educ. v. Benton*, 44 IDELR 272, 406 F. Supp. 2d 1248 (S.D. Ala. 2005) (A hearing officer found the vagueness of the child's present levels of performance in two of his IEPs to be contrary to the IDEA's requirements, and the district court agreed: "Without a clear exposition of Benton's present level of performance, [his] annual goals defined by reference to the present performance levels are unmoored, untethered and meaningless.").)

Statement of Measurable Annual Goals

The IEP must include:

> (i) A statement of measurable annual goals, including academic and functional goals designed to —

(A) Meet the child's needs that result from the child's disability to enable the child to be involved in and make progress in the general education curriculum; and

(B) Meet each of the child's other educational needs that result from the child's disability;

(ii) For children with disabilities who take alternate assessments aligned to alternate achievement standards, a description of benchmarks or short-term objectives. . . .

34 CFR 300.320(a)(2).

The district court on remand in *Deal v. Hamilton County Department of Education*, 46 IDELR 45 (E.D. Tenn. 2006), *aff'd*, 108 LRP 1858 (6th Cir. 2008), held that the unusually numerous goals and objectives in Zachary's IEPs were sufficiently specific and measurable:

In October of 1998, the IEP team met to draft [Zachary's] IEP for the 1998-1999 school year. [District] personnel suggested 78 goals, and the parents suggested 600 goals. . . . The IEP team incorporated 137 of the 600 goals recommended by the parents into [Zachary's] IEP.

. . . The goals and objectives [in the 1998-1999 IEP] are numerous and detailed. . . . Mrs. Deal agreed that the IEP included a very long and detailed set of goals and objectives. The goals cover the areas of fine motor skills, articulation, communication, readiness, receptive language, gross motor skills, behavioral skills, social skills, self-help skills, and pre-vocational skills.

. . .

. . . [In the 1999-2000 IEP, Zachary's] goals and objectives included goals in social/behavioral skills, adaptive skills, fine motor skills, gross motor skills, self-help skills, communication, pre-vocational, and readiness skills.

In contrast, the district court in *Escambia* found the district's IEP for the child in question to be inadequate, in large part because the annual goals were not measurable. The child (Benton) had received special education services in elementary school since 1997 as a child with autism. His mother, after participating in numerous IEPs for her son, became frustrated with the district's provision of services and filed a due process hearing request in 1994. Although the district court's decision does not provide much detail about the factual background of the case, the hearing officer's decision "devoted substantial attention to the conduct of Benton during the hearing itself." The description of Benton's behavior helps to illustrate some of the concerns underlying the dispute:

In particular, Benton's behaviors included "flapping his arms, repeatedly striking his chest and stomach with an open hand, making unintelligible noises, clapping and pacing around the room." He had numerous inappropriate interactions with others in the hearing room, including pulling his lawyer's hair, kissing his expert on the cheek twice, touching/rubbing the Hearing Officer's head, and grabbing the shoulders of another lawyer. Upon his removal from the hearing room, Benton struck himself and subsequently burst back into the room.[1]

The hearing officer concluded, among other things, that Benton's IEPs for 2002-2003 and 2003-2004 were so deficient as to have violated the child's right to a FAPE. One deficiency noted by the hearing officer was the "paucity of meaningful benchmark records or clear, measurable goals" in these IEPs. Specifically, "the Hearing Officer deemed the 'annual goals' section of the IEP flawed because it did not identify measurable goals, but cryptically referred to an 80% accuracy objective, without delineating 'what the Petitioner was to attain eighty percent accuracy in.'"

The district court agreed. Contrary to the school district's assertion that the procedural defects in the IEP did not result in a denial of FAPE, the court quoted the hearing officer's statement that "in the absence of meaningful, measurable goals and objectives, there can be no 'appropriate and meaningful education and developmental interventions for a child with autistic spectrum disorder.'" The court continued, explaining that the combined IEP deficiencies

> were no trivial, trifling technicalities; to the contrary, the defects in Benton's IEP went to the suitability of the overall education program. . . . [W]ithout meaningful, measurable objectives and goals, Benton's educators and parents were engaged in a futile endeavor to pin the tail on a moving donkey while blindfolded in a dark room. In other words, meaningful, measurable objectives give Benton a target to work towards and his educators and parents a way to evaluate his progress. The mushy, ambiguous, unquantifiable goals often listed in Benton's IEPs are at odds with IDEA objectives to have Benton progress towards tangible goals and measure his achievement in working towards them. Vague and unmeasurable objectives are the handmaiden of stagnation, as a program cannot possibly confer an educational benefit to Benton if his teachers and parents do not know where they are trying to take Benton and how they will know when he has arrived.
>
> . . . [T]he [district] has couched Benton's annual goals in fuzzy, ambiguous, ill-defined terms that render it difficult to know what the objectives are, and virtually impossible to measure whether he has achieved them.

Description of How Goals Will Be Measured

The IEP must contain a description of:

> (i) How the child's progress toward meeting the annual goals . . . will be measured; and
>
> (ii) When periodic reports on the progress the child is making toward meeting the annual goals (such as through the use of quarterly or other periodic reports, concurrent with the issuance of report cards) will be provided. . . .

34 CFR 300.320(a)(3).

Measuring progress on the child's IEP goals is a critical component of ensuring FAPE because it enables school officials and the parent to monitor the extent to which the child is receiving a meaningful educational benefit, and thus whether or not the IEP needs to be revised. In the *Escambia* case discussed above, the court found that Benton's IEP was undermined by both a lack of measurable annual goals and the "lack of notations as to whether Benton had mastered any of his benchmarks. . . ." The record demonstrated that the student's IEPs for 2002-2003 and 2003-2004 "lacked any record of dates of mastery" of the IEP goals and objectives. The court noted:

> According to the Hearing Officer, the mastery dates shortcoming was "[t]he most glaring deficiency" in the IEPs, and was significant because the absence of dates of mas-

tery prevented parents or other IEP team members from ascertaining Benton's progress during the school year.

Despite the district's assertion that the IEP's procedural defects did not adversely affect Benton, the court strongly disagreed:

> But the Hearing Officer plainly found adverse impacts on Benton. Where dates of mastery are either excluded from IEPs or jotted in as a pro forma afterthought at year's end, the IEP team "cannot determine the progress that the child has been making during the school year" towards achieving annual goals and whether adjustments to the program might be necessary. . . . Because these observations and findings go directly to the Hearing Officer's special expertise in educational matters and because such determinations are clear, well-developed, well-reasoned and well-supported, the undersigned finds that they are entitled to deference.
>
> . . . Needless to say, it would be extraordinarily difficult for meaningful programs to be fashioned prospectively for Benton without reasonable records to demonstrate where he had been and what he had previously had and had not been able to achieve. From an educational standpoint, Benton's teachers, counselors and parents desperately needed the diagnostic, evaluative tool of dates of mastery to understand Benton's status and needs. The omission of such information must necessarily have a detrimental effect on educational programs formed and implemented for Benton on a going forward basis, inasmuch as such programs would be based on imperfect (and/or simply missing) data about Benton's achievement.

The court held that the failure to provide measurable annual goals in the IEP, and to adequately measure Benton's progress toward mastery of the annual goals, contributed to a denial of FAPE for him.

(*See also Board of Educ. of County of Kanawha v. Michael M.*, 95 F. Supp. 2d 600 (S.D. W. Va. 2000) (The school district was unable to persuade the court that its challenged IEPs were reasonably calculated to provide a FAPE for the child, partly because the progress documentation was not sufficiently tied to the goals and objectives to be meaningful. For example, testimony from the child's kindergarten teacher "regarding [his] success and progress that he achieved during the year . . . lacked any direct reference to the IEPs or to particular examples of connections between the goals and objectives in the IEP and methodology contained therein." Similarly, the student's autism mentor "monitored [the child's] progress during the school year through the use of checklists and a notebook . . . [but] offered no testimony concerning the creation and initial implementation of the IEP and the reasons, if any, for adopting the methodology for the purpose of accomplishing the goals that [the child] has attained. Instead, she merely monitored [his] progress, but had no way of determining the source of that progress.").)

In the absence of accurate and consistently measured progress data, the likelihood increases that an inappropriate IEP may be "recycled" year after year — a practice that is neither educationally sound nor legally defensible. In the case of *County School Board of Henrico County, VA v. R.T.*, 45 IDELR 274, 433 F. Supp. 2d 657 (E.D. Va. 2006), discussed throughout this book, the court expressed strong disapproval of the school district's lack of responsiveness to the parents' concerns about RT's unsatisfactory rate of progress using the district's TEACCH methodology. Although the parents expressed concern to district personnel that the district's IEP recycled a methodology and goals that had (according to the parents) failed to help RT make progress in the past, the district apparently ignored their concerns. When the parents then brought a legal challenge against the district on this issue, the district's failure to accurately measure the child's progress rendered it unable to defend itself against the parents' claims.

In particular, when the dispute reached federal district court, the court considered evidence presented by the school district of RT's purported progress while enrolled at Twin Hickory. However, the court found that the testimony of the district's key witness in this regard, RT's teacher (Ms. Butler), was less than credible — in no small part because her reports of his progress, documented only with after-the-fact, anecdotal information, were flatly contradicted by the parents' reports after observing RT in her class:

> Ms. Butler . . . testified that RT occasionally engaged in stimming, but could physically attend for up to 30 minutes. She also stated that his visual attendance improved from one second to three or four seconds in the several weeks he was at Twin Hickory. Ms. Butler recorded RT's work on his goals at the end of each day and sent notes home to inform the parents about each child's progress. . . . Based on her notes, Ms. Butler expressed the opinion that RT had made progress in her class. However, the Court finds that Ms. Butler's assessment of RT is entitled to little weight because it is based on anecdotal, rather than systematic, data collection.

> . . .

> [In addition, while observed in class one day by his parents, RT demonstrated minimal attending, imitation and communication skills and displayed stimming behaviors throughout almost the entire school day. For example,] [w]hen the parents arrived . . . the children were seated together in a circle. The teacher sought to make each student respond to commands such as "stand up," "arms up," and the like. RT was sitting in his chair but not paying any attention to the circle activities and instead staring up at a fluorescent light, stereotypic activity in which almost all the witnesses testified he often engaged. . . .

> After circle, Ms. Butler had to escort RT to the PECS stand, assist RT with the PECS cards, and lead RT to the one-on-one station. At the one-on-one station, RT continued to stare at the lights and Ms. Butler did not redirect his attention. Ms. Butler attempted to get RT to make animal noises, but RT did not respond. RT was supposed to play with a peg-board, but instead he stared at the light and rubbed his hands over the peg board. Ms. Butler did not redirect RT's attention.

> Following that activity, RT was led to a computer where he was supposed to interact with the computer using a mouse. However, Mrs. T. testified the computer program was non-interactive. Instead, RT sat there by himself for a few minutes clicking to no avail on the screen until he became distracted, turned the mouse over and began stimming by stroking the mouse ball and running his hands over the texture of a computer speaker. [Other witnesses] also observed this stereotypical desire for tactile self-stimulation.

> At snack time, RT was given his lunch box by the aide. The students are supposed to open their own lunch boxes and, using PECS, choose what snack they want. RT did not open his lunch box, and was unable to use the PECS system to communicate what he wanted to choose and eat. After trying unsuccessfully to get a response, the aide chose for RT and he ate. Ms. Butler then asked the children to throw their snack refuse in the trash. RT did not respond. After further prompting and direction, Ms. Butler took RT to the trash can and Ms. Butler had RT throw the trash out by directing his arms and hands. RT was then seated at an individual work station with a puzzle and left on

his own for ten minutes. RT did not engage with the puzzle. Instead, he stared at the beams of sunlight coming through one of the station's partitions. No teacher redirected his attention.

RT's mother also "testified that she never observed Ms. Butler writing down any data." The parents therefore found it unbelievable when, at the end of the above-described day, Ms. Butler sent home a note stating that "RT had finished two puzzles with minimal prompting and practiced the tiger roar sound."

This district's approach of "recycling" an inappropriate IEP was a significant factor in the court's conclusion that it had violated the IDEA. And, instead of deferring to the district's preferred TEACCH methodology, the court held that "RT required a highly structured, highly focused education methodology such as ABA therapy in which RT would receive intensive one-on-one instruction." Had the district taken more care to accurately and consistently measure RT's progress toward his IEP goals, it may have been possible to make adjustments to RT's program that would have ensured his progress. The court concluded that RT's lack of progress was the result of the TEACCH methodology; however, a more timely recognition of his lack of progress may have led to adjustments in the implementation of the methodology without necessitating a change in the methodology. (*See also M.S. & Simchick v. Fairfax County Sch. Bd.*, 47 IDELR 289 (E.D. Va. 2007) (The court affirmed the hearing officer's conclusion that because challenged IEPs from 2002-2005 were substantially similar in key respects to a 2001-2002 IEP under which the student made "no notable progress," the challenged IEPs were not reasonably calculated to provide FAPE.); *Board of Educ. of County of Kanawha v. Michael M.*, 95 F. Supp. 2d 600, 609 n.8 (S.D. W. Va. 2000) ("Although a school district can meet its statutory obligation even though its IEP proves ultimately unsuccessful, the fact that the program is unsuccessful is strong evidence that the IEP should be modified during the development of the child's next IEP. Otherwise, the new IEP would not be reasonably calculated to provide educational benefit in the face of evidence that the program has already failed.").)

The court's disapproval of the teacher's "anecdotal" data collection in *County School Board of Henrico County, VA v. R.T.* raises another important issue in the arena of methodology disputes for students with autism spectrum disorders. The IDEA does not specify how progress toward a child's IEP goals must be documented. The USDE states in its comments to the revised IDEA 2004 regulations:

> The specific times that progress reports are provided to parents *and the specific manner and format in which a child's progress toward meeting the annual goals is reported* is best left to State and local officials to determine.

71 Fed. Reg. 46,664 (2006) (emphasis added).

Some courts have explicitly recognized the IDEA's silence on this issue in rulings that uphold a district's chosen approach to progress documentation against parents' demands for more "objective" or "systematic" (e.g., DTT-style) documentation. For example, in *J.P. ex rel. Popson v. West Clark Community Schools*, 38 IDELR 5, 230 F. Supp. 2d 910 (S.D. Ind. 2002), discussed elsewhere in this book, the parents requested that the district provide ABA methodology for their son, as well as "charts and logs indicating J.P.'s progress" (i.e., the type of charts and logs that are maintained specifically as an integral component of ABA therapy[2]). The hearing officer ruled in favor of the parents regarding their progress documentation request, but the district court disagreed:

> If the Hearing Officer meant to suggest that it was reasonable to expect West Clark's teachers to provide charts and logs in an ABA/DTT format, then the Court disagrees.

That would be tantamount to requiring the teachers to use discrete trial training, so they could "chart" J.P.'s progress in terms of the percentage of successful trials. *Given the Hearing Officer's holding that it was not mandatory for the school to use an ABA/ DTT model for teaching J.P., it seems unlikely that the Hearing Officer meant to hold that ABA/DTT recording methods must be used.*

On the other hand, if the Hearing Officer merely meant that [the district] should be sensitive to the parents' "reasonable" desire for frequent and detailed information about J.P.'s progress and activities in school, the Court agrees. But the record shows that [the district] provided ample information in other formats, including school-home notebooks and formal progress reports rating percentage of improvement towards desired goals. [The district's] expert . . . testified that there was ample information in these reports, by which J.P.'s progress could be measured. The Popsons did not present any testimony, expert or otherwise, to the contrary. Therefore, the Court finds that the Popsons were kept abreast of J.P.'s progress.

Nevertheless, the Popsons complain that these forms of evaluation were not objective enough, presumably meaning in the clinical sense that they did not contain reports of successes and failures in performing discrete repeatable events. *But the IDEA does not require such scientific objectivity; it merely requires honest and thorough reports of progress.* (Emphases added.)

As discussed in Chapter 8, the IDEA does not require that the IEP team specify the methodology in the IEP. Instead, it is the USDE's position that the IEP team need only specify a methodology or methodologies when necessary to ensure a FAPE. Progress monitoring and documentation are essential features of many of the methodologies widely utilized with children with autism spectrum disorders. When the IEP team specifies a methodology in a child's IEP, school districts should take care to ensure that the methodology is implemented with fidelity, including any progress monitoring and documentation component. Moreover, even in those situations where a child's IEP does not specify a methodology, failure to measure and document progress in a manner that is systematic, thorough and meaningful is one of the types of comprehensive programming failures that, as we have emphasized throughout this book, can render a district's methodology selection more vulnerable to legal challenge. The *Henrico County* case discussed above illustrates this point, as the court's ruling in favor of the parents on the methodology dispute issue was based in part on its finding that the district's progress documentation was unreliable and insufficient.

Statement of Special Education and Related Services

The IEP must include:

A statement of the special education and related services and supplementary aids and services, based on peer-reviewed research to the extent practicable, to be provided to the child, or on behalf of the child, and a statement of the program modifications or supports for school personnel that will be provided to enable the child —

(i) To advance appropriately toward attaining the annual goals;

(ii) To be involved in and make progress in the general education curriculum in accordance with paragraph (a)(1) of this section, and to participate in extracurricular and other nonacademic activities; and

(iii) To be educated and participate with other children with disabilities and nondisabled children in the activities described in this section. . . .

34 CFR 300.320(a)(4).

The requirement that the special education and related services must be "based on peer-reviewed research to the extent practicable" was extensively discussed in Chapter 4. The growing consensus regarding the components of a comprehensive program of special education and related services for children with autism spectrum disorders was extensively discussed in Chapter 3. While these decisions must be individualized, as emphasized in Chapter 4 (on predetermination) and Chapter 7 (on preparation versus predetermination), school districts must enter the IEP team process with a good understanding of the research regarding the full range of special education and related service needs of children with autism spectrum disorders. With this background, district personnel will be alert to the ways in which each individual child's needs might trigger the array of services appropriate for children with autism spectrum disorders. The following are some examples:

- A child with an autism spectrum disorder might need the related service of counseling or social work services to address skill deficits in the areas of behavior and social interaction. *See, e.g., W.C. by Sue C. v. Cobb County Sch. Dist.*, 44 IDELR 273, 407 F. Supp. 2d 1351 (N.D. Ga. 2005), in which the court found that the district's provision of social skills supports and strategies provided educational benefit to a child with Asperger's Disorder:

  > To improve his behavioral development, the Plaintiff also participated in a weekly social skills group, led by a social worker. The students watched videos, had discussions, received instruction, and participated in role playing exercises to improve their social skills. The Plaintiff was also allowed to use a computer game to match emotions with facial expressions. The Plaintiff had the further opportunity to practice these social skills in the community during monthly field trips designed to reinforce principles that were being taught in class. For example, the class went to the grocery store to learn about measurements and to the book store to learn about reference materials.

- A child with an autism spectrum disorder might need special education or related services to facilitate the generalization of skills and to maintain functional use of these skills. *See, e.g., Thompson R2-J v. Luke P.*, 48 IDELR 63 (D.C. Colo. 2007), in which the court found that the district failed to provide the necessary in-home or community-based training to address Luke's need to generalize learned skills, and instead made only a few recommendations regarding specific methods the parents might try at home. The court was persuaded by the following findings of the hearing officer:

  > [E]ducating Luke required addressing Luke's difficulty with generalizing learned skills, his tendency towards regression, his need to overcome social and communication difficulties, and his academic problems. The hearing officer also concluded that Luke's education required special emphasis on his daily life and self care skills, including sleeping, eating, toilet training, and engaging in elementary communication and appropriate behaviors, which had to be functional outside of the school environment. Although the IEP developed by the Berthoud team ad-

dressed substantive aspects of his autism, social and communication problems, and mental retardation, the hearing officer opined that the skills would not be transferred and the IEP did not address Luke's problems with regression. The hearing officer noted that Luke "will derive no benefit at all from attaining goals and objectives in school if he cannot replicate any of his accomplishments anywhere else. The skills involved are not embellishments and frills. They are the most basic ingredients to social functioning, such as eating, sleeping, dressing, toilet training, communicating, and proper behavior."

- In the case of *W.S. ex rel. C.S. v. Rye City School District*, 46 IDELR 285, 454 F. Supp. 2d 134 (S.D.N.Y. 2006), the court upheld the district's proposed IEP for a child with an autism spectrum disorder. This IEP provided an array of uniquely tailored services to meet the child's needs as described below:

> The District's [Committee on Special Education ("CSE")] met on July 13, 2004 to discuss . . . the recently-completed FBA and the recommendations of the private evaluators. [The parents] and their attorney attended the meeting. The CSE also reviewed the child's speech-language triennial evaluation, a subsequent March 2004 Occupational Therapy report, and the November 2003 triennial psychological and educational evaluations. After reviewing these inputs, the IEP that had been proposed in April was modified by reducing the student to staff ratio in the first grade special class to reflect anticipated enrollment (from 8:1+2 to 6:1+2); adding a requirement that C.S. would receive a minimum of 60 minutes of instruction per day to meet language needs (which would occur during her time in the first grade special education classroom); increasing the frequency of parent training to 30 minutes per week; adding a speech-language consultation with the parents for an hour a month; adding a special education consultation for two hours per week in order to provide a liaison for services and consultation in behavior management and instructional modification for the regular first grade classroom teacher.

Transition Services

As the 2001 National Research Council Report states, autism "generally has life-long effects on how children learn to be social beings, to take care of themselves, and to participate in the community."[3] As a result, transition services are likely to be a pivotal component of IEPs for older children with autism spectrum disorders.

The requirement for transition services is stated in the IDEA regulations as follows:

> *Transition services.* Beginning not later than the first IEP to be in effect when the child turns 16, or younger if determined appropriate by the IEP Team, and updated annually, thereafter, the IEP must include —
>
> (1) Appropriate measurable postsecondary goals based upon age appropriate transition assessments related to training, education, employment, and, where appropriate, independent living skills; and
>
> (2) The transition services (including courses of study) needed to assist the child in reaching those goals.

34 CFR 300.320(b).

The case of *Mr. I. ex rel. L.I. v. Maine School Administration District No. 55*, 47 IDELR 121, 480 F.3d 1 (1st Cir. 2007), discussed earlier, illustrates the way in which an autism spectrum disorder can undermine a child's chances for achieving adult independence, including further education and employment, unless appropriate special education services and supports are provided. That case involved a student with Asperger's Disorder who excelled academically in elementary school until fourth or fifth grade. At that point, her academic performance began to decline somewhat, and she also started to display sadness, anxiety, and problems in her peer relationships. This period of increasing turbulence culminated in her suicide attempt when she was in sixth grade.

As noted in Chapter 2, after this crisis, LI was diagnosed with Asperger's Disorder, adjustment disorder and depressed mood. The school district maintained, however, that her disability did not adversely affect her educational performance, and that therefore she was not eligible for special education services under the IDEA. The parents challenged the school district in a due process hearing and then on appeal before a district court and the 1st Circuit Court of Appeals, where they prevailed.

One of the reasons that LI was determined by the court to qualify for IDEA services was that evidence demonstrated that "a number of LI's symptoms . . . hindered her in" the area of preparation for employment. In particular, a private social worker who provided LI with counseling testified that, "without social skills coaching, LI is unlikely to master the flexible thinking, problem solving, teamwork, and communication abilities she will need for employment in the future." The court analyzed both the IDEA and relevant state law and regulations, concluding that "educational performance" includes more than just academics under the law:

> Maine's broad definition of "educational performance" [which includes academic and non-academic areas (including "daily life activities, mobility, etc.")] squares with the broad purpose behind the IDEA: "to ensure that all children with disabilities have available to them a free and appropriate public education that emphasizes special education and related services designed to meet their unique needs and prepare them for further education, *employment*, and *independent living*." 20 USC 1400(d)(1)(A) (emphases added). We have likewise held that the IDEA entitles qualifying children to services that "target '*all* of [their] special needs,' whether they be academic, physical, emotional, or social."

The court also noted that "'career preparation' . . . comprises one of the 'content standards dictated by [state] statute" in Maine, and observed that "the IDEA exists, in part, to ensure children with disabilities receive an education preparing them for employment." Based on the foregoing analysis, the court determined that the fact that "a number of LI's symptoms have hindered her in this area . . . was itself an adequate basis [upon which to conclude] that LI's educational performance has suffered."

When deciding whether to address the transition needs of a child with an autism spectrum disorder prior to the child turning age 16 (since the regulation provides, "or younger if determined appropriate"), school districts should be mindful of the many difficulties that children with autism spectrum disorders face in acquiring and generalizing the skills necessary for a successful transition to postsecondary life. One key skill area is that of independence. The case of *A.C. and M.C. on behalf of M.C. v. Board of Education of the Chappaqua Central School District*, 47 IDELR 294 (S.D.N.Y 2007), illustrates the importance of addressing the child's need to learn independence early on.

M.C., who attended a district elementary school from preschool through fourth grade, was eligible for services under the IDEA due to his multiple disabilities, including "'Pervasive Developmental Disorder (PDD), significant language disabilities, significant learning disabilities, motor development issue[s], and sensory dysfunction, including visual defects and auditory processing difficulties.'" He was considered high functioning within the diagnostic category of autistic disorder; however, he displayed various significant areas of need, such as a:

marked attention deficit [that] compromise[d] his cognitive, academic, behavioral and social functioning . . . a short attention span, poor social skills, and [he] was easily distracted by extraneous stimuli. His adaptive behaviors, i.e., daily living skills, communication and socialization, were below age expectant levels. Projective tests suggested that [he was] easily overwhelmed by emotional or complex stimuli. . . .

In addition, I.Q. tests conducted when he was 9 years old "indicated that [his] performance . . . was hindered by severe attention and executive function deficits as well as significant language processing difficulties."

During M.C.'s fourth-grade year (2003-2004), the district provided him with a "'co-teaching support program,' in which [he] was educated within the general education environment with special education support," including services from a special education teacher and assistant and a full-time 1:1 aide.

The district's proposed IEP for M.C. for his fifth-grade year (2004-2005) called for a

> full-time 6:1 co-teaching support program in the general education environment with a full-time (5:1) program assistant. The IEP also called for daily integrated individual math instruction and daily individual reading instruction in a separate location, along with occupational therapy and psychological consultation.

During the IEP development process for fifth grade, M.C.'s parents expressed concern about their son's progress and raised the issue of placing him in a private school, but the district maintained that its proposed IEP was appropriate. The parents disagreed, so they rejected the district's proposed IEP and filed a request for a due process hearing, alleging that the district's IEP was "substantively flawed" and thus denied M.C. a FAPE.

The hearing officer agreed with the parents, but that decision was subsequently reversed by an administrative review officer. However, on appeal to federal district court, the court also ruled in favor of the parents, concluding that the school district had, in fact, denied M.C. a FAPE.

The parents claimed in pertinent part that the district's IEP was faulty because its "'goals and objectives were inappropriate and failed to promote M.C.'s independence and progress.'" In particular, they asserted that providing him with a 1:1 aide "without attempting to increase his independence and ability to function without that help. . . . 'essentially kept M.C. in a state of learned helplessness,' and even caused M.C. to regress." In response, the district argued that the IEP was appropriate, and had been "developed by experienced educators who sought to balance the goals of allowing M.C. to remain in the middle school with his peers, with his needs for individualized attention."

Although the court acknowledged that the district provided substantial support to M.C., it agreed with the parents and the hearing officer that

> "the constant presence of a 1:1 aide may be viewed as a crutch or palliative measure, especially where, as here, lack of independence is one of the student's most significant deficits. The 1:1 aide may have been very inhibiting in the proposed middle school placement, where he or she would have followed [M.C.] from class to class."

> [The district's] *failure to address the need to increase [M.C.'s] independence* conforms to the pattern of "learned helplessness" that was being fostered by the District's IEP. This approach is epitomized by the District's designation of a separate bathroom facility for M.C., and the fact that the District admitted that *there was no "instruction goal aimed to have M.C. use a community bathroom." By failing to address M.C.'s need to increase his independence*, and indeed by fostering "learned helplessness" through the *indefinite use* of a 1:1 aide, the Court concludes that the IEP was substantively inadequate and not reasonably calculated [to] provide M.C. with a FAPE. (Emphases added.)

The court's ruling suggests that although the school district recognized M.C.'s need for substantial support, it only fulfilled part of its obligation under the IDEA by putting that support in place. As this case illustrates, districts should be alert to the fact that a child's high level of need for certain special education supports may also indicate a related need to achieve greater independence from those supports over time. This is just one example of the degree of sensitivity and careful balancing that the IEP team must bring to bear during the IEP development process.

The deference ordinarily shown to school districts in a methodology dispute can be compromised as a result of material inadequacies in the IEP. The IDEA specifies what must be included in a child's IEP. With a strong full and individual evaluation to guide the IEP team, the team must carefully construct an IEP that contains all of the required components. Resting on a full and individual evaluation, and considering all of the required information including special factors, the IEP is built from the foundation up: present levels, annual goals, special education and related services. Once these determinations are made, the team is well-positioned to make an appropriate determination about the child's placement. The IEP team must ask: "What is the least restrictive environment in which to implement the child's IEP?" Chapter 10 addresses key issues of concern with respect to placement for children with autism spectrum disorders in the least restrictive environment.

ENDNOTES

[1] *Excambia County Bd. of Educ. v. Benton*, 44 IDELR 272, 406 F. Supp. 2d 1248 (S.D. Ala. 2005).

[2] "Discrete trial training (DTT) is a method of instruction in which tasks are broken down into small sub-tasks, instruction is given on each individual sub-task, and positive reinforcement is given for correct answers. DTT entails frequent repetition of drills set up in a programmed sequence. The results can be measured with objective data, noting the number of trial successes." (*Id.* at 928 (internal citations omitted).)

[3] National Research Council (2001). *Educating children with autism*. 11. Committee on Educational Interventions for Children with Autism. Catherine Lord and James P. McGee, eds. Division of Behavioral and Social Sciences and Education. Washington, D.C.: National Academy Press.

113

Chapter 10

Placement and Least Restrictive Environment

Just as a child's full and individual evaluation should drive the development of an IEP based on the child's needs, the process of IEP development (including all required components) should drive the determination of the child's educational placement. The IDEA requires that each child eligible for special education services must be educated in the least restrictive environment (LRE) that is appropriate to meet his or her needs.

Each public agency must ensure that —

(i) *To the maximum extent appropriate*, children with disabilities, including children in public or private institutions or other care facilities, are educated with children who are nondisabled; and

(ii) Special classes, separate schooling, or other removal of children with disabilities from the regular educational environment occurs only if the nature or severity of the disability is such that education in regular classes with the use of supplementary aids and services can not be achieved satisfactorily.

34 CFR 300.114(a)(2). (Emphasis added.)

In determining the educational placement of a child with a disability, including a preschool child with a disability, each public agency must ensure that —

(a) The placement decision —

(1) Is made by a group of persons, including the parents, and other persons knowledgeable about the child, the meaning of the evaluation data, and the placement options; and

(2) Is made in conformity with the LRE provisions of this subpart . . .;

(b) The child's placement —

(1) Is determined at least annually;

(2) Is based on the child's IEP; and

(3) Is as close as possible to the child's home;

(c) Unless the IEP of a child with a disability requires some other arrangement, the child is educated in the school that he or she would attend if nondisabled;

(d) In selecting the LRE, consideration is given to any potential harmful effect on the child or on the quality of services that he or she needs; and

(e) A child with a disability is not removed from education in age-appropriate

115

regular classrooms solely because of needed modifications in the general education curriculum.

34 CFR 300.116.

LRE considerations for children with autism spectrum disorders are not fundamentally different than those for children with other disabilities:

> *Least Restrictive Environment.* As much as possible, children with disabilities must be educated with children without disabilities. The educational philosophy is to move children with special needs as close to the normal setting (regular classroom) as feasible. For a child with an autistic spectrum disorder, this means that there is an expectation that the child should be interacting on a regular basis with children without autism, if at all possible, and within a regular classroom, with reverse mainstreaming or in other supervised settings. When recommending another placement, a school must explain in writing why a child is not being placed in a regular classroom.[1]

The Legal Standard

Unlike the mandate of a free appropriate public education, which (as explained in Chapter 1) was interpreted by the U.S. Supreme Court in *Rowley*, the U.S. Supreme Court has not interpreted the least restrictive environment mandate. Instead, most of the circuits have interpreted the mandate and adopted its own standard and/or factors for how LRE determinations should be made and evaluated, or adopted the standard and/or factors of another circuit. Therefore, when determining least restrictive environment issues for a particular student, IEP teams must be careful to follow the applicable standard and/or factors in making these decisions.

The 1st Circuit Standard (RI, MA, NH, ME, PR)

The 1st Circuit Court of Appeals has not articulated or adopted a clearly delineated standard or set of factors to indicate how LRE determinations should be made, other than to state that districts must take both the LRE mandate and the FAPE mandate into consideration when making placement determinations. (*See, e.g., Roland M. v. Concord Sch. Committee*, 16 IDELR 1129 (16 EHLR 1129), 910 F.2d 983, 993 (1st Cir. 1990) ("Correctly understood, the correlative requirements of educational benefit and least restrictive environment operate in tandem to create a continuum of educational possibilities. To determine a particular child's place on this continuum, the desirability of mainstreaming must be weighed in concert with the [IDEA's] mandate for educational improvement. Assaying an appropriate educational plan, therefore, requires a balancing of the marginal benefits to be gained or lost on both sides of the maximum benefit/least restrictive fulcrum. Neither side is automatically entitled to extra ballast.").)

The 2d Circuit Standard (NY, VT, CT)

The 2d Circuit Court of Appeals has not articulated or adopted a specific standard or set of factors governing LRE determinations.

The 3d Circuit Standard (PA, NJ, DE, VI)

The 3d Circuit Court of Appeals in *Oberti v. Board of Education of Borough of Clementon School*, 19 IDELR 908, 995 F.2d 1204 (3d Cir. 1993*)*, adopted the 5th Circuit standard in *Daniel R.R. v. SBOE*, 441 IDELR 433 (441 EHLR 433), 874 F.2d 1036 (5th 1989), except that the 3d Circuit held that the school district has the burden of proving compliance with the IDEA's least restrictive environment mandate.[2] (See the discussion of *Daniel R.R.* below.)

The 4th Circuit Standard (WV, VA, NC, SC, MD)

The 4th Circuit Court of Appeals in *DeVries v. Fairfax County School Board*, 441 IDELR 555 (EHLR 441:555), 882 F.2d 876 (4th Cir. 1989), adopted the 6th Circuit standard set forth in *Roncker v. Walter*, 554 IDELR 381 (EHLR 554:381), 700 F.2d 1058 (6th Cir. 1983), *cert. denied*, 464 U.S. 864 (1983). (See the discussion of *Roncker* below.)

The 4th Circuit *DeVries* case involved a 17-year-old child with autism named Michael. Prior to this dispute, Michael had been attending a private day school for children with disabilities. His mother sought placement for Michael at his home high school campus. After first recommending continued placement at the private day school, the district recommended a segregated vocational center, 13 miles from home, and located on a regular high school campus. His mother challenged the recommendation of the school district to place Michael at the Vocational Center. The due process hearing officer, review officer and district court upheld the school district's placement. The 4th Circuit also upheld the child's placement at the Vocational Center, affirming the district court's comparison of the two placement options.

The 4th Circuit acknowledged that mainstreaming is not appropriate for every child with a disability. The court observed that Michael exhibited child-like behaviors, had difficulty with social interaction, and became agitated in response to change. The court described his cognitive and academic functioning as "depressed." In applying the *Roncker* standard to the facts of this case, the 4th Circuit, discussing the lower court's findings, noted:

> "[T]here is no appropriate peer group academically, socially or vocationally for Michael at Annandale [his home high school campus]."

> Even with an aide to assist him in comprehending and in communicating with teachers and students, the court found that "Michael would simply be monitoring classes" with nonhandicapped students at Annandale.

> [Michael's] disability would make it difficult for him to bridge the "disparity in cognitive levels" between him and the other students, he would glean little from the lectures, and his individualized work would be at a much lower level than his classmates.

> In contrast, . . . the South County Vocational Center, located within a public high school, would provide a structured program with the one-to-one instruction that Michael requires, including appropriate instruction in academic subjects, vocational and social skills, community-based work experiences, and access to all the programs and facilities of the public high school.

The 5th Circuit Standard (TX, LA, MS)

The 5th Circuit Court of Appeals articulated its standard including factors for consideration in *Daniel R.R. v. SBOE*, 441 IDELR 433 (EHLR 441:433), 874 F.2d 1036 (5th Cir. 1989). As its standard, the court articulated a two-part test: (1) Can education in the regular classroom with the use of supplemental aids and services be achieved satisfactorily? (2) If the answer is no, and the school district intends to remove the child from the regular education setting, has the district mainstreamed the child to the maximum extent appropriate?

The court identified five factors for consideration when reviewing an LRE dispute: (1) whether the district has taken steps to accommodate the child with disabilities in regular education (by providing supplementary aids and services or modifying its regular education program); (2) whether these efforts were sufficient or token (because, although the requirement that districts modify and supplement regular education is broad, districts need not provide every conceivable supplementary aid or service to assist the child); (3) whether the child will receive an educational benefit from regular education; (4) the child's overall educational experience in the mainstreamed environment, balancing the benefits of regular and special education (since, on the one hand, the nonacademic benefit that the child receives from mainstreaming may tip the balance in favor of mainstreaming, even if the child cannot flourish academically; while on the other hand, placing the child in regular education may be detrimental to the child); and (5) the effect the disabled child's presence has on the regular classroom environment.

The 6th Circuit Standard (MI, OH, KY, TN)

The 6th Circuit Court of Appeals articulated its standard and factors for consideration in *Roncker v. Walter*, 554 IDELR 381 (EHLR 554:381), 700 F.2d 1058 (6th Cir. 1983), *cert. denied*, 464 U.S. 864 (1983). The case involved a child, Neill Roncker, who was 9 years old and severely mentally retarded. He also suffered from a seizure disorder. Due to his level of cognitive functioning, he required constant supervision to ensure his safety. Neill was not considered dangerous. Following a period of attendance on a campus that allowed for him to have contact with nondisabled children, the school district proposed a placement in an entirely segregated county school. The district staff believed that this environment would be academically superior for Neill. During the pendency of the dispute, Neill began attending a class for severely retarded children on a regular elementary school campus where he had limited opportunities during lunch, gym, and recess to interact with nondisabled peers. At trial, the parties agreed that Neill should not be instructed in a regular classroom setting. Instead, the dispute was narrowly tailored to the issue of his opportunity to have contact with nondisabled peers.

The 6th Circuit articulated the following standard:

> In a case where the segregated facility is considered superior, the court should determine whether the services which make that placement superior could be feasibly provided in a non-segregated setting. If they can, the placement in the segregated school would be inappropriate under the Act.

The factors the court identified for consideration were: (1) whether the child made progress in the integrated setting; and if the child did not make progress, whether there were additional services that would have improved his performance; (2) a comparison of the benefits of regular and special education (with the segregated placement being appropriate if any marginal benefits received from mainstreaming are far outweighed by the benefits gained from services, which could not feasibly be provided in the non-segregated setting); (3) whether the child is disruptive in the non-segregated setting; (4) cost (since excessive spending on one disabled child deprives other disabled children); "[c]ost is no defense, however, if the school district has failed to use its funds to provide a proper continuum of alternative placements for handicapped children."

The 7th Circuit Standard (WI, IL, IN)

The 7th Circuit Court of Appeals in *Beth B. v. Van Clay*, 36 IDELR 121, 282 F.3d 493 (7th Cir. 2002), *cert. denied*, 537 U.S. 948 (2002), declined to adopt a standard, stating: "Each student's educational situation is unique. We find it unnecessary at this point in time to adopt a formal test for district courts uniformly to apply when deciding LRE cases. The Act itself provides enough of a framework for our discussions."

As noted previously in this book, the case of *Beth B.* involved a girl with Rett Syndrome, a disorder within the spectrum of autism disorders, who began receiving special education services from the district when she was 2 years old. The court described the impact of her disability as follows:

> Beth is nonverbal; she uses an instrument called an eye gaze, a board with various pictures and symbols that she singles out with eye contact, to communicate her wants and needs, as well as other communication devices that allow her to choose among symbols or to hear messages recorded by others. She relies on a wheelchair for mobility. She, like nearly all Rett sufferers, has an extreme lack of control over body movement. Although her mental capacity is difficult to assess precisely, due to her extreme communicative and motor impairments, some experts contend that she has the cognitive ability of a twelve-to-eighteen-month old infant. Others estimate that she has the ability of a four-to-six-year old. She is unable to read or recognize numbers.

In kindergarten, she was placed by parent request in a regular education class with extensive special education and support services, and her IEP team met annually thereafter "to review and update" her IEP. Following her second-grade year, however, the district determined that a different placement would provide more educational benefit than she was able to receive in the regular education setting, and it recommended that she be placed in a self-contained Educational Life Skills (ELS) classroom in a neighboring district. The proposed setting was described by the court as follows:

> [It] would be located in a public school building and would serve students between the ages of six and twenty one with mild, moderate, or severe handicaps. Generally, six to eight students comprise one ELS classroom, and the student-teacher ratio is one-to-one. ELS students in the program are mainstreamed into regular education classrooms during music, library, art, computer, and certain social studies and science classes, and join other students at the school during lunch, recess, assemblies, and field trips. Additionally, reverse mainstreaming is employed; that is, regular education students come into the ELS classroom to allow for interaction between ELS and non ELS students.

Beth's parents rejected this proposal because they preferred the full-time regular education placement for Beth, and they filed a request for a due process hearing to challenge the district's proposal. Under the "stay-put" provision of the IDEA, Beth remained in a regular education setting during the course of the due process hearing (at which the district prevailed) and the parents' subsequent appeal to federal court. At the time of the parents' later appeal to the 7th Circuit, Beth was in a seventh-grade regular education class. Her educational experience in the regular classroom was described by the Circuit Court as follows:

> Students in the seventh grade attend six 42-minute classes a day. They have three-minute passing periods between class. Beth's aides help her travel from room to room during the passing periods, although it is extremely difficult for her to do so in such a short time frame. Since the first grade, Beth has worked with a one-on-one aide at all times and has used an individualized curriculum tied in subject matter, as much as possible, to that of the other students in the class. Beth's current curriculum is geared toward someone at a preschool level. When her peers worked on mathematics, she was exposed to various numbers. When the class studied meteorology and weather patterns, she looked at pictures of clouds. Beth cannot participate in class discussions or lectures.

The 7th Circuit affirmed the ruling of the lower court (and that of the due process hearing officer) in the school district's favor. The 7th Circuit stated that under the IDEA, a school district must provide [eligible] children with a free appropriate public education ("FAPE") together, to the maximum extent appropriate, with nondisabled children ("least restrictive environment" or "LRE"). The FAPE provision and LRE provision are two sides of the same IEP coin. The first requirement is absolute and focuses on the school district's proposed placement — here, the ELS program; the second is relative and concentrates on other placement options — here, keeping Beth in the regular classroom. The LRE requirement shows Congress's strong preference in favor of mainstreaming, *but does not require, or even suggest, doing so when the regular classroom setting provides an unsatisfactory education.* (Emphasis added.)

The court characterized the parents' argument follows: "So long as the regular classroom confers 'some educational benefit' to Beth . . . the school district cannot remove her from that setting."

The court rejected the argument, stating, "This language is misplaced." Instead, the court agreed with the school district's position, "that a modicum of developmental achievement does not constitute a satisfactory education."

The court concluded that the program proposed by the district for Beth constituted mainstreaming to the maximum extent appropriate. In particular, the court stated that the district's provision of "reverse mainstreaming opportunities, as well as time spent with nondisabled peers" in a variety of settings, offered "an acceptable point along the 'continuum of services' between total integration and complete segregation," demonstrating the district's "concern both for [Beth's] development and for keeping her mainstreamed[ ] to an appropriate extent."

Early on, the district had recognized Beth's lack of achievement in the regular education setting and had appropriately determined that this placement was not appropriate for her. Its ELS proposal, in contrast, offered Beth the chance to have numerous mainstreaming opportunities as well as an appropriate level of special education services and supports to meet her needs.

The 8th Circuit Standard (ND, SD, NE, MN, IA, MO, AR)

The 8th Circuit Court of Appeals in *A.W. v. Northwest R-1 School District*, 558 IDELR 294 (EHLR 558:294), 813 F.2d 158 (8th Cir. 1987), *cert. denied*, 484 U.S. 847 (1987), adopted the 6th Circuit standard in *Roncker*. (See the above discussion of *Roncker*.)

The 9th Circuit Standard (CA, AK, HI, OR, WA, NV, ID, MT, AZ)

The 9th Circuit Court of Appeals in *Sacramento City Unified School District v. Rachel H.*, 20 IDELR 812, 14 F.3d 1398 (9th Cir. 1994), *cert. denied*, 512 U.S. 1207 (1994), adopted four factors for consideration that employed elements from both the *Daniel R.R.* and *Roncker* standards as follows: (1) the educational benefits available in a regular classroom, supplemented with appropriate aids and services, as compared with the educational benefits of a special education classroom; (2) the non-academic benefits of interaction with children who were not disabled; (3) the effect of the child's presence on the teacher and other children in the classroom; and (4) the cost of mainstreaming the child.

The 10th Circuit Standard (CO, NM, UT, WY, KS, OK)

The 10th Circuit Court of Appeals in *L.B. v. Nebo School District*, 41 IDELR 206, 379 F.3d 966 (10th Cir. 2004), adopted the 5th Circuit standard set forth in *Daniel R.R.* (See the above discussion of *Daniel R.R.*)

The *Nebo* case involved K.B., a child with an autism spectrum disorder. The parents requested that the school district provide an aide for K.B. at her private, entirely mainstreamed preschool, coupled with 40 hours per week of at-home ABA programming at public expense. The district instead offered placement at Park View Special Education Preschool with an additional eight to 15 hours per week of ABA. "Park View is populated mainly by disabled students, but includes thirty to fifty percent typically developing children ('typical children') who are present for the full length of the preschool classes." The district offered to increase the ratio to 50 percent for K.B., but the parents declined this proposal.

The parents filed a request for a due process hearing seeking reimbursement for the provision of K.B.'s supplementary aide and the cost of her ABA program, which consisted of the following: "(1) forty hours per week of ABA services; (2) seven and one-half hours per week of preparation time for ABA therapists to plan for individual sessions; (3) two and one-half hours per week for a team meeting with K.B.'s five ABA therapists; (4) one day per month for an ABA consultant to train the five therapists; (5) materials for ABA program; (6) one hour of speech therapy per week; and (7) occupational therapy as needed." The due process hearing officer ruled in favor of the school district. The district court upheld the hearing officer's decision. The parents appealed.

The 10th Circuit reversed the lower court's decision. What is troubling for school districts about this reversal is that the Circuit Court treated the case as a placement rather than a methodology dispute. The following statements by the 10th Circuit reveal how this characterization allowed a comparison of the two methodologies to determine which one was superior from a least restrictive environment standpoint, avoiding altogether whether the district's methodology conferred a FAPE:

> [T]his court concludes that Park View was not K.B.'s least restrictive environment. Because this conclusion establishes a violation of the IDEA's substantive LRE provision, this court need not address whether Nebo provided K.B. with a FAPE.

> Thus, the LRE requirement is a specific statutory mandate. It is not, as the district court in this case mistakenly believed, a question about educational methodology.

> Thus, this case turns on the first prong of the *Daniel R.R.* LRE test (i.e., whether education in the regular classroom, with the use of supplementary aides and services, can be achieved satisfactorily).

> A preponderance of the evidence shows that the academic benefits which K.B. derived from the mainstream classroom, are greater than those she would have received in Park View's classroom. Despite the hearing officer's contrary conclusion, the evidence shows that K.B. was succeeding in the mainstream classroom with the assistance of her aide and intensive ABA program.

The 11th Circuit Standard (AL, GA, FL)

The 11th Circuit Court of Appeals in *Greer v. Rome City School District*, 18 IDELR 412, 950 F.2d 688 (11th Cir. 1991), *withdrawn on other grounds*, 956 F.2d 1025 (11th Cir. 1992); *reinstated in part per curiam*, 967 F.2d 470 (11th Cir. 1992), adopted the 5th Circuit standard in *Daniel R.R.* (See the *Daniel R.R.* discussion above.)

The D.C. Circuit Standard

The LRE cases of the D.C. Circuit Court of Appeals track both the statutory and regulatory language of the IDEA, and neither adopt the standards established by other circuits nor articulate their own standard.

"Full Inclusion" under the IDEA

The IDEA regulations continue to require a continuum of placements:

(a) Each public agency must ensure that a continuum of alternative placements is available to meet the needs of children with disabilities for special education and related services.

(b) The continuum required in paragraph (a) of this section must —

(1) Include the alternative placements listed in the definition of special education under §300.38 (instruction in regular classes, special classes, special schools, home instruction, and instruction in hospitals and institutions); and

(2) Make provision for supplementary services (such as resource room or itinerant instruction) to be provided in conjunction with regular class placement.

34 CFR 300.115.

The USDE Office of Special Education and Rehabilitative Services (OSERS) states with regard to the continuum of placements:

Part B recognizes . . . that children with disabilities may need to be educated in various types of settings in order to meet their unique educational needs.

Placement cannot be based solely on such factors as the category of the child's disability, the availability of appropriate staff, administrative convenience, or the configuration of the service-delivery system.

We emphasize that Part B requires that each child with a disability must be educated in the LRE in which that child's unique educational needs can best be met. In all cases, the determination of what constitutes each child's LRE must be made on a case-by-case-basis in accordance with the requirements outlined above.[3]

With regard to the concept of "full inclusion" in a regular education setting for all children with disabilities, OSERS cautions:

This emphasis on the *individual* [in the name "Individuals with Disabilities Education Act"] is in keeping with all of the provisions of the Act, and with its very spirit. . . . It was clearly the intent of the Congress in passing this law that decisions about the provision of services, including the decision about where those services are provided, would be made on a case-by-case basis, depending on the needs of each individual child. (Emphasis in the original.)

It is important for your constituent to know that I am in full support of the integration and inclusion of children and adults with disabilities in schools and in the community alongside their nondisabled peers. I have frequently expressed my strong belief that *all* students with disabilities are entitled to have a full continuum of educational placement options made available to them. I also believe that all students have a right to be integrated in an educational program in the least restrictive environment (LRE) that appropriately meets their unique needs.

While Part B does not use the term "inclusion," it does require placement in the LRE appropriate to the child['s] needs.

[I]nnovations in practice which have emerged from the projects supported under [OS-ERS'] discretionary programs have facilitated both improvements in the quality of services delivered to students in integrated educational settings, and the development of creative and effective supports to enable increased numbers of students with disabilities to be served in regular classroom settings.[4]

LRE Considerations for Children with Autism Spectrum Disorders

Although LRE considerations for children with autism spectrum disorders are not fundamentally different than those for children with other disabilities, there are certain issues and potential areas of dispute that arise with more frequency than others in the context of methodology disputes for children with these disorders. This is because of some of the unique characteristics of the disability that present barriers to learning.

Certain characteristics of children with autism spectrum disorders can significantly hinder the acquisition of new skills, often creating a need for more restrictive placements. As noted by the court in the case of *County School Board of Henrico County, VA v. R.T.*, 45 IDELR 274, 433 F. Supp. 2d 657 (E.D. Va. 2006):

"The main characteristics that differentiate autism from other developmental disorders include 'behavioral deficits in eye contact, orienting to one's name, joint attention behaviors (e.g., pointing, showing), pretend play, imitation, nonverbal communication, and language development.'" Many autistic children appear to have tuned the world out and are in their own worlds, not paying attention to others or engaging in normal social interactions.

The case of *Pachl v. Seagren*, 46 IDELR 1, 453 F.3d 1064 (8th Cir. 2006), illustrates how these characteristics and needs implicate placement. The case involved a girl named Sarah who had a number of physical and developmental disabilities, one of which was autism spectrum disorder. While in elementary school she attended "an integrated mainstream classroom" for most of each day, except for time spent in PT, OT, and SLP sessions. When she began middle school, however, the district proposed that she spend a significant portion of the school day in a self-contained special education classroom. Her parents objected to the idea and asked that Sarah be observed by an outside expert in the special education setting to evaluate its appropriateness. The district allowed the observation by the expert, whose resulting report recommended a regular education setting with individually tailored supports for most of the school day for Sarah, rather than the district's proposed special education placement:

[The expert believed] that [this special education setting] limited "age appropriate interaction and communication skills," and that the tasks Sarah . . . was asked to perform [there] were "non-functional in nature and of little or no use to future functioning." [The expert] also criticized the mainstream time as lacking effective inclusive practices and "characterized by missed opportunities for learning new skills, using her present skills, working on her IEP goals, or interacting with her age mates."

Based on information from the expert's report as well as the parents' input, the district proposed a new IEP. The new IEP included the following components:

[It] increased [Sarah's] mainstream classroom time to approximately 280 minutes each day and limited the time in the [special education] classroom to approximately 120 minutes per day. The School District also implemented some of [the expert's] suggestions for integrating Sarah among her peers, such as providing a more age-appropriate schedule book and reading materials and placing her locker nearer to the homeroom classroom. The School District, however, declined to follow [the expert's] recommendation that Sarah not spend any time in the [special education] classroom. Finding that recommendation to be in conflict with the assessments of other experts who had observed Sarah, the IEP team concluded that she *"need[s] to have skills presented to her in a repetitive and structured manner"* and that she *"has shown progress in response to these strategies."* (Emphasis added.)

Despite the extensive changes to the district's proposed IEP, Sarah's parents maintained that they wanted Sarah's hours in the self-contained classroom eliminated altogether. Because the school district and the parents could not reach agreement as to which placement was the least restrictive environment appropriate for Sarah, the district filed a request for a due process hearing to resolve this matter (as well as other issues).

The hearing officer ruled in favor of the district, as did the federal district court that reviewed the administrative decision. The district court concluded:

[T]he hearing officer did not err when finding that the School District proved that the combination of mainstream and [special education] learning environments will provide Sarah a meaningful education in the least restrictive environment.

In their subsequent appeal to the 8th Circuit Court of Appeals, Sarah's parents reiterated their assertion that the district's proposed IEP violated the IDEA's LRE requirement because it did not allow Sarah to spend 100 percent of her school time in a regular classroom. In analyzing this issue, the court cited to the standard it had articulated in an earlier case:

[W]e have emphasized that the statutory language [in the IDEA] "significantly qualifies the mainstreaming requirement by stating that it should be implemented 'to the maximum extent *appropriate*,' and that it is inapplicable where education in a mainstream environment 'cannot be achieved *satisfactorily*.'" Thus, removing a child from the mainstream setting is permissible when "the handicapped child would not benefit from mainstreaming," when "any marginal benefits received from mainstreaming are far outweighed by the benefits gained from services which could not feasibly be provided in the non-segregated setting," and when "the handicapped child is a disruptive force in the non-segregated setting." (Emphasis in original.)

The 8th Circuit upheld the lower court's conclusion that a fully mainstreamed setting was not the appropriate placement for Sarah because it would not offer meaningful educational benefit to her, even with the provision of extensive supports and services:

The district court . . . [found] that "[w]ith full inclusion, Sarah would be among her peers, but not learning with them." The court believed that "[p]lacing her in a learning environment in which she is inundated with lectures and instructions that she does not understand and which have no relevance to the work she is capable of doing is not providing her with a meaningful education."

In contrast, the court concluded that the special education setting proposed by the district was the only place where certain instructional strategies could be provided to Sarah that would target her areas of need and provide her with meaningful educational benefit:

The educators who work with Sarah reported that structured teaching, which includes "establishing routines, using a visual schedule and work system, and using a visual structure to clarify independent work tasks," was a sound education strategy that was aimed at helping Sarah develop greater independence. Sarah's service providers also believed that the functional skills that Sarah would need to develop personal independence could not be fully addressed in the mainstream environment, "since many of the functional skills that Sarah should learn cannot be performed in the natural setting of the mainstream with enough frequency to provide her the needed practice."

While some children with autism spectrum disorders often need more restrictive placements for acquisition of new skills, some also may often be appropriately educated in less restrictive settings for the reinforcement and generalization of learned skills. In the case of *Gill v. Columbia 93 School District*, 31 IDELR 29 (W.D. Mo. 1999), the court approved of the district's well-planned combination of placements. The parents sought an "intensive adult-led one-on-one instruction for Matthew for most of the day." The district offered "a structured classroom-based curriculum with significant one-on-one instruction for Matthew within that environment." The parents complained that the district's program represented "an inconsistent 'patchwork' of placements." The court upheld the district's IEP and placement, stating:

Under the IDEA, the school district must work at integrating Matthew into the school environment. To do that, they must make sure that Matthew has all the skills to function within that environment. It is documented that Matthew has learned to adapt to the classroom environment and that he can function and participate in school-type activities. This is not a case where the child is nonfunctional at school.

The court specifically addressed the parents' concerns regarding the "patchwork of placements" as follows:

The "patchwork" of placements of which plaintiffs complain are, in fact, *discrete placements designed to meet Matthew's specific educational needs.* The [district's] IEP offers several instructional environments *geared specifically to Matthew's educational needs* and was calculated to provide him with educational benefit. (Emphases added.)

While certain characteristics of children with autism spectrum disorders can significantly hinder the acquisition of new skills, thereby creating a need for more restrictive placements, the need to be educated in less restrictive settings for the reinforcement and generalization of learned skills can be an equally compelling consideration. As the cases in this chapter illustrate, the degree to which a child with an autism spectrum disorder should be educated in an inclusive setting must be an individualized decision, and when it is determined to be appropriate, such inclusive placement must be well-designed and executed.

ENDNOTES

[1] National Research Council. (2001). *Educating children with autism*. 178-79. Committee on Educational Interventions for Children with Autism. Catherine Lord and James P. McGee, eds. Division of Behavioral and Social Sciences and Education. Washington, D.C.: National Academy Press.

[2] Note, however, that the burden of proof determination by the 3d Circuit is no longer controlling, given the U.S. Supreme Court's decision in *Schaffer v. Weast*, 44 IDELR 150, 526 U.S. 49 (2005), which allocated the burden of proving an IEP's appropriateness to the party challenging it. (*See, e.g., L.E. v. Ramsey Bd. of Educ.*, 44 IDELR 269, 435 F.3d 384 (3d Cir. 2006) (The court concluded that *Schaffer*'s holding regarding the burden of proof applies to both the FAPE and LRE components of the analysis when reviewing the appropriateness of a child's IEP.).)

[3] *See Letter to Goodling*, 18 IDELR 213 (OSERS 1991).

[4] *See Letter to Frost*, 18 IDELR 594 (OSERS 1991).

Conclusion

As stated at the outset, the goal of this book is to provide public school educators with guidelines gleaned from key cases to help prepare them to address the autism methodology debate in a manner that is both educationally sound and legally defensible. Despite the challenges posed for school districts when educating children with autism spectrum disorders, there are steps educators can take to help ensure positive results, including the following:

✓ Build a solid understanding of the nature of autism among district staff members;

✓ Design and develop a comprehensive program for children with autism spectrum disorders that contains essential components as established by the research, without regard to methodology;

✓ Consider and make knowledgeable decisions about an array of instructional methodologies to be utilized within the framework of sound, broad-based programming;

✓ Ensure appropriate levels of professional development so that staff is qualified to select, tailor, and implement an array of methodologies;

✓ Conduct a full and individual evaluation of each child suspected of or identified as having an autism spectrum disorder, as appropriate;

✓ Conduct IEP team meetings that meet the procedural and substantive requirements of the IDEA, including those requirements regarding team membership and meaningful parent participation; and

✓ Use the results of the full individual evaluation to inform the development of an individually tailored IEP for each eligible child that includes all of the required components under the IDEA and that is reasonably calculated to enable the child to receive meaningful educational benefit in the least restrictive appropriate environment.

In reviewing the case law, we have concluded that when parents prevail against school districts in autism spectrum disorder methodology disputes, it is often not due to the quality of the chosen methodologies, but rather as the result of a multitude of errors in other important aspects of identification, evaluation, educational placement, or the provision of a FAPE to the child. Fundamentally, when a methodology dispute is brought as either a single issue case or as part of a multi-issue case, school districts tend to win those disputes when they have provided sound identification, evaluation, educational placement, and the provision of a FAPE to the child. It is when a district's overall program is weak, and an autism spectrum disorder methodology dispute becomes embedded within broader challenges to that program or to key aspects of the program, that a court will allow itself to engage in a comparison of methodologies and be more likely to uphold the parent's preferred methodology over the school district's choice. By building a strong, well-considered, research-based comprehensive program from the ground up, school districts can better ensure that their individual methodology selections will be appropriate, and if challenged, will be given deference by a hearing officer or court. We respect and appreciate the efforts of public school educators who are engaged in this challenging task. We look forward to the evolving research in this area, which will provide further guidance in educating children with autism spectrum disorders.